中华人民共和国

2023年国民经济和社会发展统计公报

STATISTICAL COMMUNIQUÉ OF THE PEOPLE'S REPUBLIC OF CHINA ON THE 2023 NATIONAL ECONOMIC AND SOCIAL DEVELOPMENT

国 家 统 计 局
National Bureau of Statistics of China

2024年2月29日
February 29, 2024

中国统计出版社
China Statistics Press

图书在版编目（C I P）数据

中华人民共和国 2023 年国民经济和社会发展统计公报 = Statistical Communiqué of the People' s Republic of China on the 2023 National Economic and Social Development : 汉英对照 / 国家统计局编 . -- 北京 : 中国统计出版社 , 2024.3
ISBN 978-7-5230-0408-1

Ⅰ . ①中… Ⅱ . ①国… Ⅲ . ①国民经济发展－统计资料－公报－中国－ 2023 －汉、英②社会发展－统计资料－公报－中国－ 2023 －汉、英 Ⅳ . ① F124-66

中国国家版本馆 CIP 数据核字 (2024) 第 036407 号

中华人民共和国 2023 年国民经济和社会发展统计公报

作　　者 / 国家统计局
责任编辑 / 郭　栋
装帧设计 / 黄　晨
出版发行 / 中国统计出版社有限公司
通信地址 / 北京市丰台区西三环南路甲 6 号　邮政编码 /100073
发行电话 / 邮购（010）63376909　书店（010）68783171
网　　址 / http://www.zgtjcbs.com/
印　　刷 / 北京画中画印刷有限公司
经　　销 / 新华书店
开　　本 / 880mm×1230mm　1/16
字　　数 / 92 千字
印　　张 / 5.25
版　　别 / 2024 年 3 月第 1 版
版　　次 / 2024 年 3 月第 1 次印刷
定　　价 / 38.00 元

目录

CONTENTS

中华人民共和国
2023 年国民经济和社会发展统计公报[1]

国家统计局

2024 年 2 月 29 日

2023年是全面贯彻党的二十大精神的开局之年，是三年新冠疫情防控转段后经济恢复发展的一年。面对复杂严峻的国际环境和艰巨繁重的国内改革发展稳定任务，在以习近平同志为核心的党中央坚强领导下，各地区各部门坚持以习近平新时代中国特色社会主义思想为指导，全面贯彻落实党的二十大和二十届二中全会精神，按照党中央、国务院决策部署，坚持稳中求进工作总基调，完整、准确、全面贯彻新发展理念，加快构建新发展格局，着力推动高质量发展，全面深化改革开放，加大宏观调控力度，着力扩大内需、优化结构、提振信心、防范化解风险，国民经济回升向好，高质量发展扎实推进，现代化产业体系建设取得重要进展，科技创新实现新的突破，改革开放向纵深推进，安全发展基础巩固夯实，民生保障有力有效，社会大局和谐稳定，全面建设社会主义现代化国家迈出坚实步伐。

[1] 本公报中数据均为初步统计数。各项统计数据均未包括香港特别行政区、澳门特别行政区和台湾省。部分数据因四舍五入的原因，存在总计与分项合计不等的情况。

一、综合

初步核算，全年国内生产总值[2]1260582亿元，比上年增长5.2%。其中，第一产业增加值89755亿元，比上年增长4.1%；第二产业增加值482589亿元，增长4.7%；第三产业增加值688238亿元，增长5.8%。第一产业增加值占国内生产总值比重为7.1%，第二产业增加值比重为38.3%，第三产业增加值比重为54.6%。最终消费支出拉动国内生产总值增长4.3个百分点，资本形成总额拉动国内生产总值增长1.5个百分点，货物和服务净出口向下拉动国内生产总值0.6个百分点。分季度看，一季度国内生产总值同比增长4.5%，二季度增长6.3%，三季度增长4.9%，四季度增长5.2%。全年人均国内生产总值89358元，比上年增长5.4%。国民总收入[3]1251297亿元，比上年增长5.6%。全员劳动生产率[4]为161615元/人，比上年提高5.7%。

图1 2019-2023年国内生产总值及其增长速度

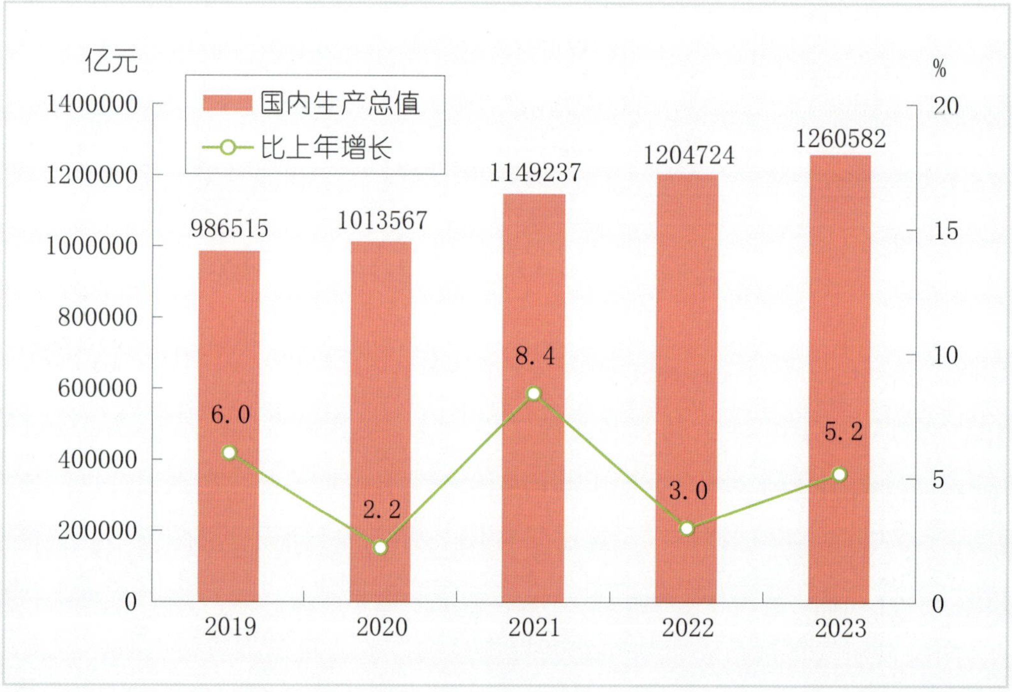

[2] 国内生产总值、三次产业及相关行业增加值、地区生产总值、人均国内生产总值和国民总收入绝对数按现价计算，增长速度按不变价格计算。

[3] 国民总收入，原称国民生产总值，是指一个国家或地区所有常住单位在一定时期内所获得的初次分配收入总额，等于国内生产总值加上来自国外的初次分配收入净额。

[4] 全员劳动生产率为国内生产总值（按2020年价格计算）与全部就业人员的比率。

图 2　2019-2023 年三次产业增加值占国内生产总值比重

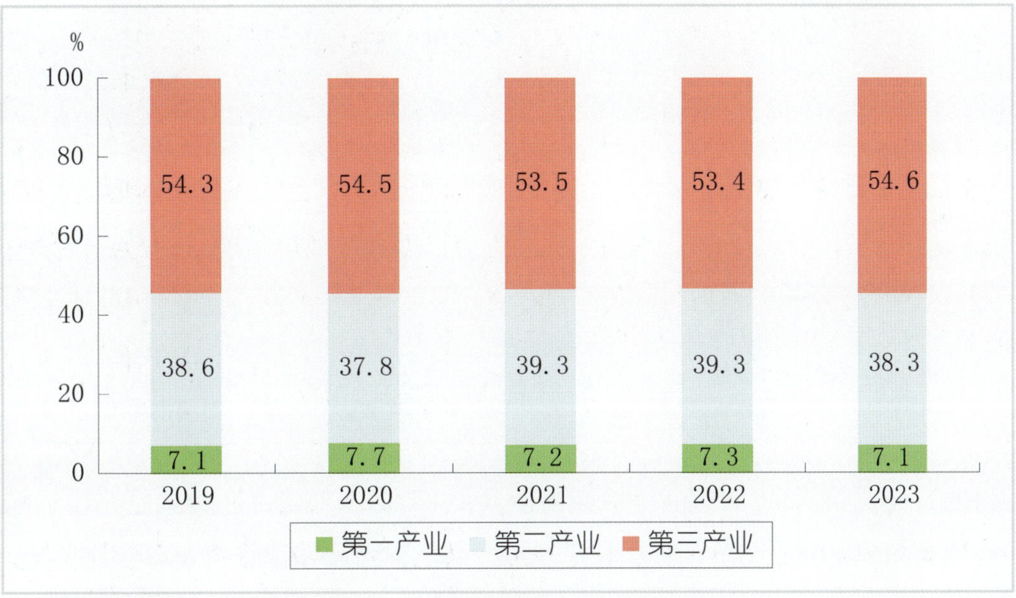

图 3　2019-2023 年全员劳动生产率

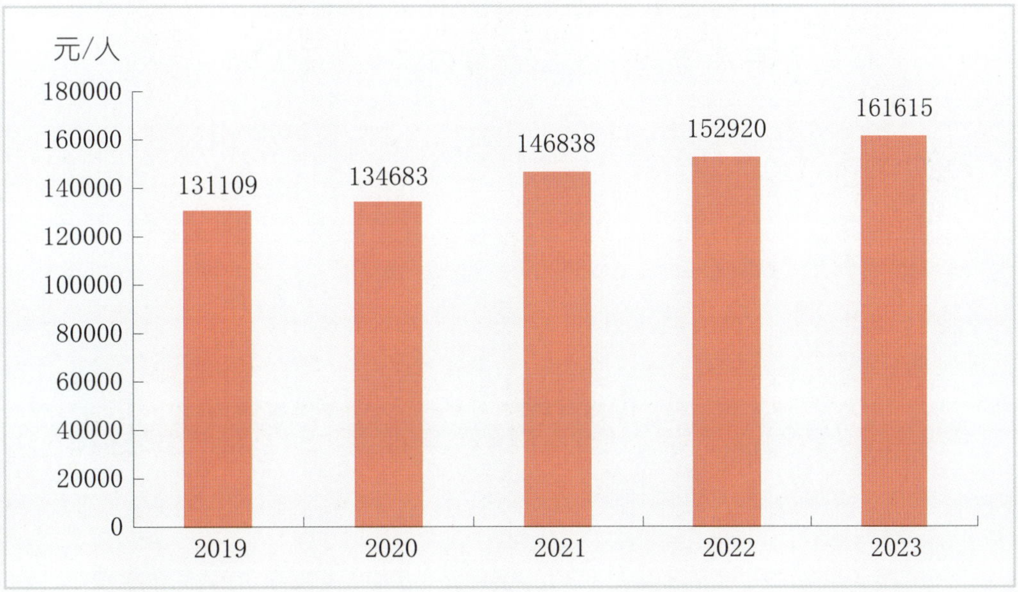

年末全国人口[5]140967万人，比上年末减少208万人，其中城镇常住人口93267万人。全年出生人口902万人，出生率为6.39‰；死亡人口1110万人，死亡率为7.87‰；自然增长率为-1.48‰。

[5] 全国人口是指我国大陆 31 个省、自治区、直辖市和现役军人的人口，不包括居住在 31 个省、自治区、直辖市的港澳台居民和外籍人员。

表1 2023年年末人口数及其构成

指 标	年末数（万人）	比重（%）
全国人口	140967	100.0
其中：城镇	93267	66.2
乡村	47700	33.8
其中：男性	72032	51.1
女性	68935	48.9
其中：0-15岁（含不满16周岁）[6]	24789	17.6
16-59岁（含不满60周岁）	86481	61.3
60周岁及以上	29697	21.1
其中：65周岁及以上	21676	15.4

年末全国就业人员74041万人，其中城镇就业人员47032万人，占全国就业人员比重为63.5%。全年城镇新增就业[7]1244万人，比上年多增38万人。全年全国城镇调查失业率平均值为5.2%。年末全国城镇调查失业率为5.1%。全国农民工[8]总量29753万人，比上年增长0.6%。其中，外出农民工17658万人，增长2.7%；本地农民工12095万人，下降2.2%。

图4 2019-2023年城镇新增就业人数

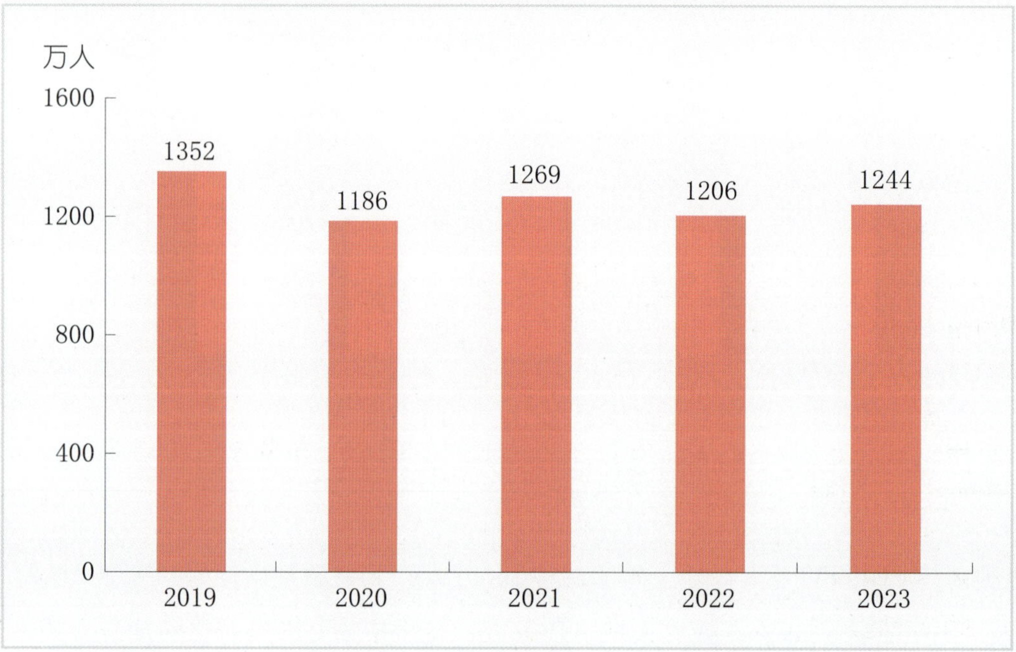

[6] 2023年年末，0—14岁（含不满15周岁）人口为23063万人，15—59岁（含不满60周岁）人口为88207万人。

[7] 城镇新增就业人数是指报告期内城镇累计新就业人员数与自然减员人数之差。

[8] 年度农民工数量包括年内在本乡镇以外从业6个月及以上的外出农民工和在本乡镇内从事非农产业6个月及以上的本地农民工。

全年居民消费价格比上年上涨0.2%。工业生产者出厂价格下降3.0%。工业生产者购进价格下降3.6%。农产品生产者价格[9]下降2.3%。12月份，70个大中城市中，新建商品住宅销售价格同比上涨的城市个数为20个，持平的为2个，下降的为48个；二手住宅销售价格同比上涨的城市个数为1个，下降的为69个。

图5 2023年居民消费价格月度涨跌幅度

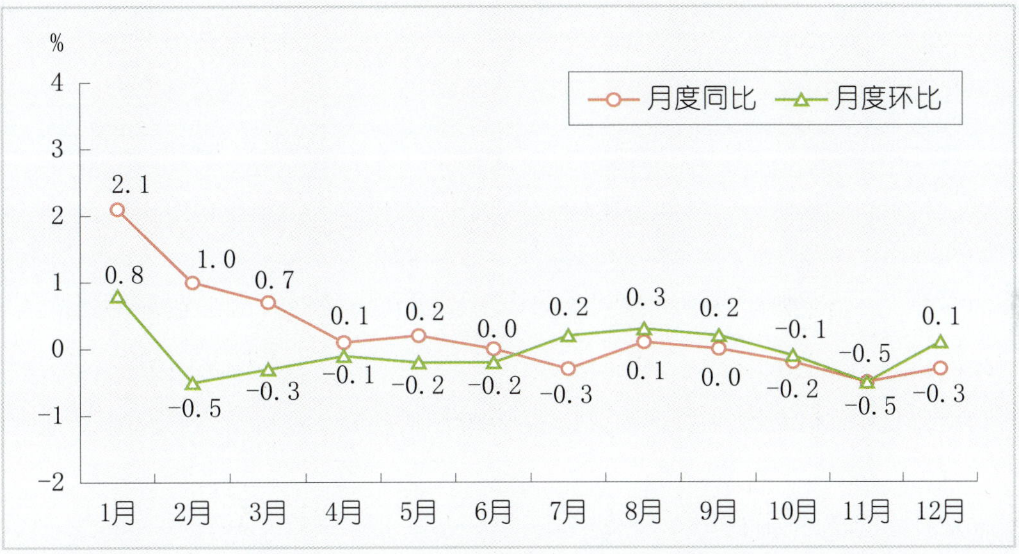

表2 2023年居民消费价格比上年涨跌幅度

单位：%

指　标	全　国	城　市	农　村
居民消费价格	0.2	0.3	0.1
其中：食品烟酒	0.3	0.4	0.1
衣着	1.0	1.1	0.6
居住[10]	0.0	0.0	0.0
生活用品及服务	0.1	0.1	-0.1
交通通信	-2.3	-2.3	-2.4
教育文化娱乐	2.0	2.1	1.5
医疗保健	1.1	1.1	1.3
其他用品及服务	3.2	3.4	2.5

[9] 农产品生产者价格是指农产品生产者第一手出售其产品时的价格。
[10] 居住类价格包括租赁房房租、住房保养维修及管理、水电燃料、自有住房服务价格。

年末国家外汇储备32380亿美元，比上年末增加1103亿美元。全年人民币平均汇率为1美元兑7.0467元人民币，比上年贬值4.5%。

图 6　2019-2023 年年末国家外汇储备

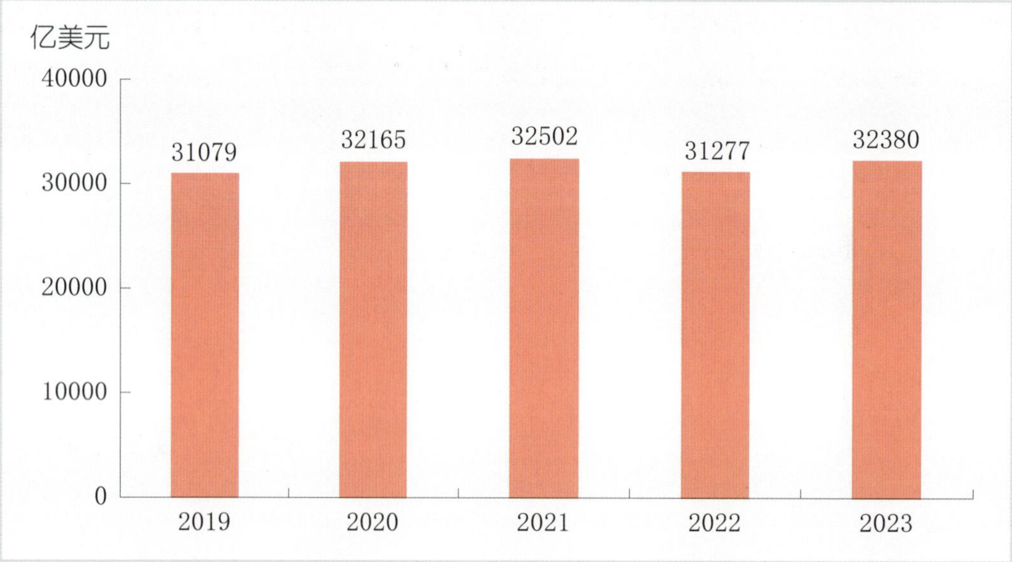

新动能成长壮大。全年规模以上工业[11]中，装备制造业[12]增加值比上年增长6.8%，占规模以上工业增加值比重为33.6%；高技术制造业[13]增加值增长2.7%，占规模以上工业增加值比重为15.7%。新能源汽车产量944.3万辆，比上年增长30.3%；太阳能电池（光伏电池）产量5.4亿千瓦，增长54.0%；服务机器人产量783.3万套，增长23.3%；3D打印设备产量278.9万台，增长36.2%。规模以上服务业[14]中，战略性新兴服务业[15]企业营业收入比上年增长7.7%。高技术产业投

[11] 由于统计调查制度规定的调查范围变动、统计执法、剔除重复数据等因素，2023 年规模以上工业相关指标增速及变化按可比口径计算。

[12] 装备制造业包括金属制品业，通用设备制造业，专用设备制造业，汽车制造业，铁路、船舶、航空航天和其他运输设备制造业，电气机械和器材制造业，计算机、通信和其他电子设备制造业，仪器仪表制造业。

[13] 高技术制造业包括医药制造业，航空、航天器及设备制造业，电子及通信设备制造业，计算机及办公设备制造业，医疗仪器设备及仪器仪表制造业，信息化学品制造业。

[14] 规模以上服务业统计范围包括：年营业收入 2000 万元及以上的交通运输、仓储和邮政业，信息传输、软件和信息技术服务业，水利、环境和公共设施管理业，卫生行业法人单位；年营业收入 1000 万元及以上的房地产业（不含房地产开发经营），租赁和商务服务业，科学研究和技术服务业，教育行业法人单位；以及年营业收入 500 万元及以上的居民服务、修理和其他服务业，文化、体育和娱乐业，社会工作行业法人单位。2023 年规模以上服务业企业财务指标增速按可比口径计算。

[15] 战略性新兴服务业包括新一代信息技术产业、高端装备制造产业、新材料产业、生物产业、新能源汽车产业、新能源产业、节能环保产业和数字创意产业等八大产业中的服务业相关行业，以及新技术与创新创业等相关服务业。

资[16]比上年增长10.3%，制造业技术改造投资[17]增长3.8%。电子商务交易额[18]468273亿元，比上年增长9.4%。网上零售额[19]154264亿元，比上年增长11.0%。全年新设经营主体3273万户，日均新设企业2.7万户。

城乡融合和区域协调发展步伐稳健。年末全国常住人口城镇化率为66.16%，比上年末提高0.94个百分点。分区域看[20]，全年东部地区生产总值652084亿元，比上年增长5.4%；中部地区生产总值269898亿元，增长4.9%；西部地区生产总值269325亿元，增长5.5%；东北地区生产总值59624亿元，增长4.8%。全年京津冀地区生产总值104442亿元，比上年增长5.1%；长江经济带地区生产总值584274亿元，增长5.5%；长江三角洲地区生产总值305045亿元，增长5.7%。粤港澳大湾区建设、黄河流域生态保护和高质量发展等区域重大战略深入推进。

图 7　2019-2023 年年末常住人口城镇化率

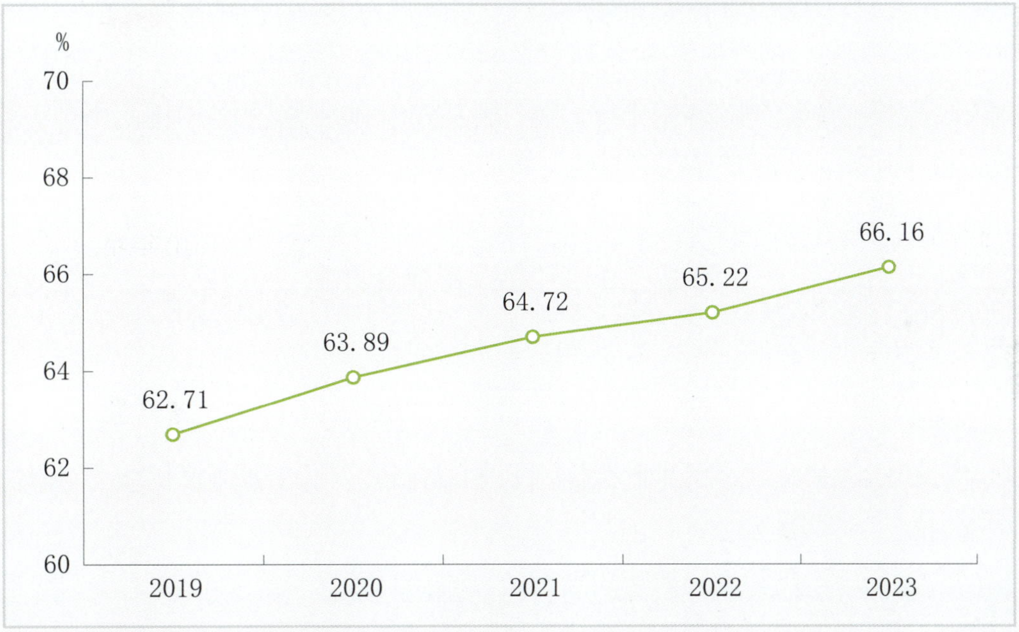

[16] 高技术产业投资包括医药制造、航空航天器及设备制造等六大类高技术制造业投资和信息服务、电子商务服务等九大类高技术服务业投资。

[17] 制造业技术改造投资是指制造业企业采用新技术、新工艺、新设备、新材料对现有设施、工艺条件及生产服务等进行改造提升所完成的投资。

[18] 电子商务交易额是指通过电子商务交易平台（包括企业自建平台和第三方平台）实现的商品和服务交易额，包括对单位和对个人交易额，2023 年增速按可比口径计算。

[19] 网上零售额是指通过公共网络交易平台（主要从事实物商品交易的网上平台，包括自建网站和第三方平台）实现的商品和服务零售额，2023 年增速按可比口径计算。

[20] 东部地区是指北京、天津、河北、上海、江苏、浙江、福建、山东、广东和海南 10 省（市）；中部地区是指山西、安徽、江西、河南、湖北和湖南 6 省；西部地区是指内蒙古、广西、重庆、四川、贵州、云南、西藏、陕西、甘肃、青海、宁夏和新疆 12 省（区、市）；东北地区是指辽宁、吉林和黑龙江 3 省。

绿色低碳转型深入推进。全年全国万元国内生产总值二氧化碳排放[21]与上年持平。水电、核电、风电、太阳能发电等清洁能源发电量31906亿千瓦时，比上年增长7.8%。在监测的339个地级及以上城市中，空气质量达标的城市占59.9%，未达标的城市占40.1%。3641个国家地表水考核断面中，水质优良（Ⅰ～Ⅲ类）断面比例为89.4%，Ⅳ类断面比例为8.4%，Ⅴ类断面比例为1.5%，劣Ⅴ类断面比例为0.7%。

二、农业

全年粮食种植面积11897万公顷，比上年增加64万公顷。其中，稻谷种植面积2895万公顷，减少50万公顷；小麦种植面积2363万公顷，增加11万公顷；玉米种植面积4422万公顷，增加115万公顷；大豆种植面积1047万公顷，增加23万公顷。棉花种植面积279万公顷，减少21万公顷。油料种植面积1392万公顷，增加78万公顷。糖料种植面积142万公顷，减少3万公顷。

全年粮食产量69541万吨，比上年增加888万吨，增产1.3%。其中，夏粮产量14615万吨，减产0.8%；早稻产量2834万吨，增产0.8%；秋粮产量52092万吨，增产1.9%。谷物产量64143万吨，比上年增产1.3%。其中，稻谷产量20660万吨，减产0.9%；小麦产量13659万吨，减产0.8%；玉米产量28884万吨，增产4.2%。大豆产量2084万吨，增产2.8%。

图8 2019-2023年粮食产量

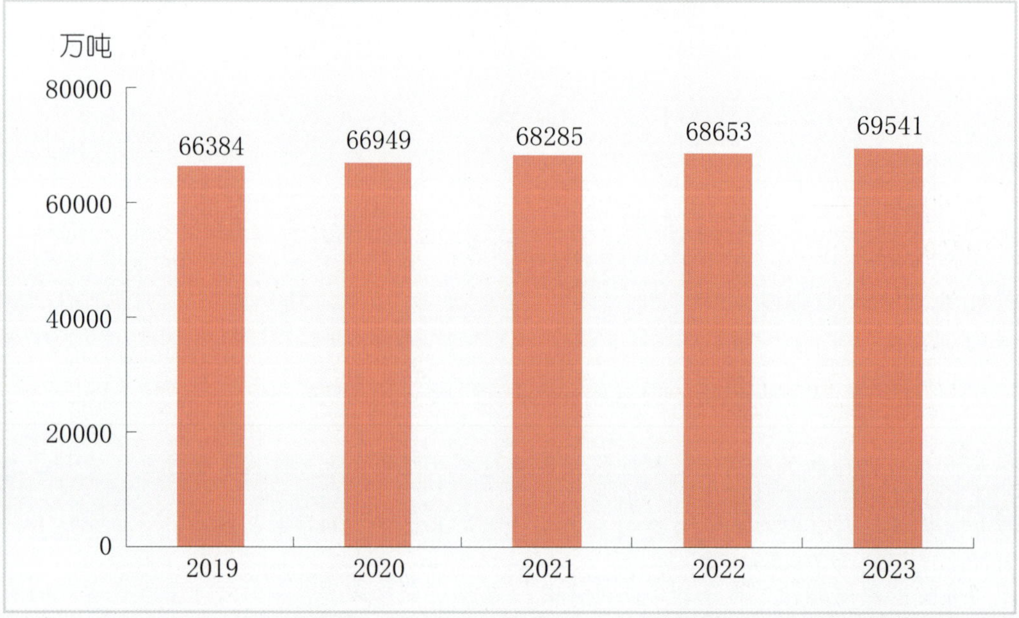

[21] 万元国内生产总值二氧化碳排放按2020年价格计算。

全年棉花产量562万吨，比上年减产6.1%。油料产量3864万吨，增产5.7%。糖料产量11504万吨，增产2.4%。茶叶产量355万吨，增产6.1%。

全年猪牛羊禽肉产量9641万吨，比上年增长4.5%。其中，猪肉产量5794万吨，增长4.6%；牛肉产量753万吨，增长4.8%；羊肉产量531万吨，增长1.3%；禽肉产量2563万吨，增长4.9%。禽蛋产量3563万吨，增长3.1%。牛奶产量4197万吨，增长6.7%。年末生猪存栏43422万头，比上年末下降4.1%；全年生猪出栏72662万头，比上年增长3.8%。

全年水产品总产量7100万吨，比上年增长3.4%。其中，养殖产量5812万吨，增长4.4%；捕捞产量1288万吨，下降1.0%。

全年木材产量11944万立方米，比上年下降2.0%。

全年新建和改造提升高标准农田面积574万公顷，新增高效节水灌溉面积164万公顷。

三、工业和建筑业

全年全部工业增加值399103亿元，比上年增长4.2%。规模以上工业增加值增长4.6%。在规模以上工业中，分经济类型看，国有控股企业增加值增长5.0%；股份制企业增长5.3%，外商及港澳台商投资企业增长1.4%；私营企业增长3.1%。分门类看，采矿业增长2.3%，制造业增长5.0%，电力、热力、燃气及水生产和供应业增长4.3%。

图 9　2019-2023 年全部工业增加值及其增长速度

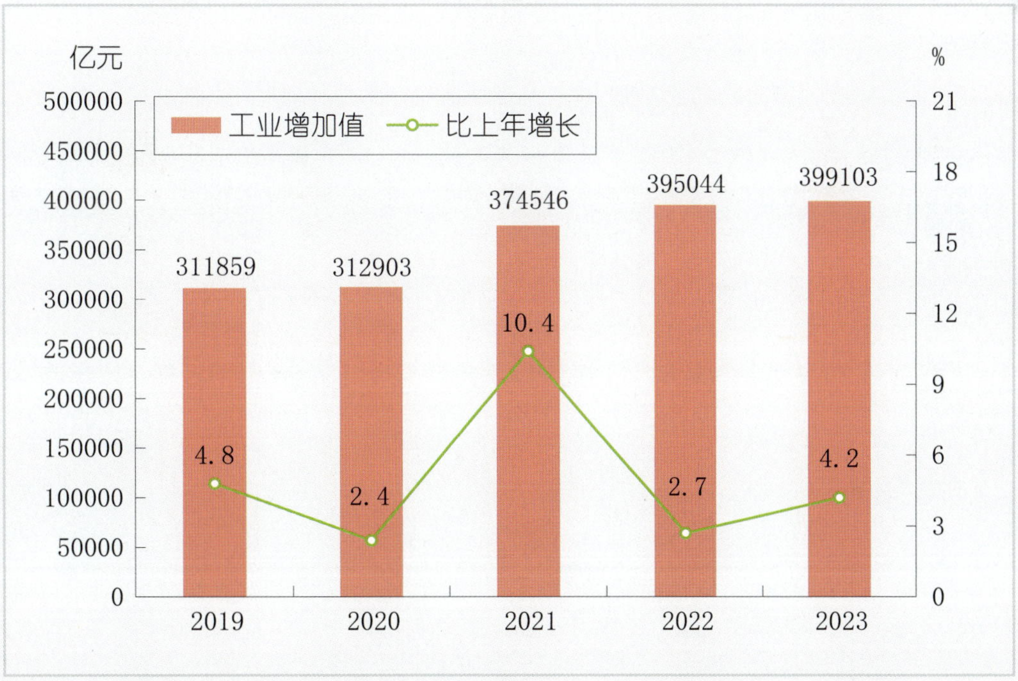

全年规模以上工业中，农副食品加工业增加值比上年增长0.2%，纺织业下降0.6%，化学原料和化学制品制造业增长9.6%，非金属矿物制品业下降0.5%，黑色金属冶炼和压延加工业增长7.1%，通用设备制造业增长2.0%，专用设备制造业增长3.6%，汽车制造业增长13.0%，电气机械和器材制造业增长12.9%，计算机、通信和其他电子设备制造业增长3.4%，电力、热力生产和供应业增长4.3%。

表3 2023年规模以上工业主要产品产量及其增长速度[22]

产品名称	单位	产量	比上年增长（%）
纱	万吨	2234.2	-2.2
布	亿米	294.9	-4.8
化学纤维	万吨	7127.0	10.3
成品糖	万吨	1270.6	-13.2
卷烟	亿支	24427.5	0.4
彩色电视机	万台	19339.6	-1.3
家用电冰箱	万台	9632.3	14.5
房间空气调节器	万台	24487.0	13.5
粗钢	万吨	101908.1	0.0
钢材[23]	万吨	136268.2	5.2
十种有色金属	万吨	7469.8	7.1
其中：精炼铜（电解铜）	万吨	1298.8	13.5
原铝（电解铝）	万吨	4159.4	3.7
水泥	亿吨	20.2	-0.7
硫酸（折100%）	万吨	9580.0	3.4
烧碱（折100%）	万吨	4101.4	3.5
乙烯	万吨	3189.9	6.0
化肥（折100%）	万吨	5713.6	5.0
发电机组（发电设备）	万千瓦	23442.7	28.5
汽车	万辆	3011.3	9.3
其中：新能源汽车	万辆	944.3	30.3
大中型拖拉机	万台	38.0	-7.2
集成电路	亿块	3514.4	6.9
程控交换机	万线	507.0	-42.6
移动通信手持机	万台	156642.2	6.9
微型计算机设备	万台	33056.9	-17.4
工业机器人	万套	43.0	-2.2
太阳能工业用超白玻璃	万平方米	159264.8	58.6
充电桩	万个	287.8	36.9

[22] 见注释[11]。
[23] 钢材产量数据中含企业之间重复加工钢材。

全年规模以上工业企业利润76858亿元，比上年下降2.3%。分经济类型看，国有控股企业利润22623亿元，比上年下降3.4%；股份制企业56773亿元，下降1.2%，外商及港澳台商投资企业17975亿元，下降6.7%；私营企业23438亿元，增长2.0%。分门类看，采矿业利润12392亿元，比上年下降19.7%；制造业57644亿元，下降2.0%；电力、热力、燃气及水生产和供应业6822亿元，增长54.7%。规模以上工业企业每百元营业收入中的成本为84.76元，比上年增加0.04元；营业收入利润率为5.76%，下降0.20个百分点。年末规模以上工业企业资产负债率为57.1%，比上年末下降0.1个百分点。全年规模以上工业产能利用率[24]为75.1%。

初步核算，全年一次能源生产总量48.3亿吨标准煤，比上年增长4.2%。

表 4　2023 年主要能源产品产量及其增长速度

产品名称	单　位	产　量	比上年增长（%）
原煤	亿吨	47.1	3.4
原油	万吨	20902.6	2.1
天然气	亿立方米	2324.3	5.6
发电量	亿千瓦时	94564.4	6.9
其中：火电[25]	亿千瓦时	62657.4	6.4
水电	亿千瓦时	12858.5	-4.9
核电	亿千瓦时	4347.2	4.1
风电	亿千瓦时	8858.7	16.2
太阳能发电	亿千瓦时	5841.5	36.7

年末全国发电装机容量291965万千瓦，比上年末增长13.9%。其中[26]，火电装机容量139032万千瓦，增长4.1%；水电装机容量42154万千瓦，增长1.8%；核电装机容量5691万千瓦，增长2.4%；并网风电装机容量44134万千瓦，增长20.7%；并网太阳能发电装机容量60949万千瓦，增长55.2%。

全年建筑业增加值85691亿元，比上年增长7.1%。全国具有资质等级的总承包和专业承包建筑业企业利润8326亿元，比上年增长[27]0.2%，其中国有控股企业4019亿元，增长4.3%。

[24] 产能利用率是指实际产出与生产能力（均以价值量计量）的比率。企业的实际产出是指企业报告期内的工业总产值；企业的生产能力是指报告期内，在劳动力、原材料、燃料、运输等保证供给的情况下，生产设备（机械）保持正常运行，企业可实现并能长期维持的产品产出。

[25] 火电包括燃煤发电量，燃油发电量，燃气发电量，余热、余压、余气发电量，垃圾焚烧发电量，生物质发电量。

[26] 少量发电装机容量（如地热等）公报中未列出。

[27] 建筑业企业利润增速按可比口径计算。报告期数据与上年已公布的同期数据之间存在不可比因素，不能直接相比计算增速。主要原因是：①加强数据质量审核，剔除主营业务不属于建筑业的相关数据。②加强统计执法检查，对发现的问题数据按照相关规定进行了改正。

图 10 2019-2023 年建筑业增加值及其增长速度

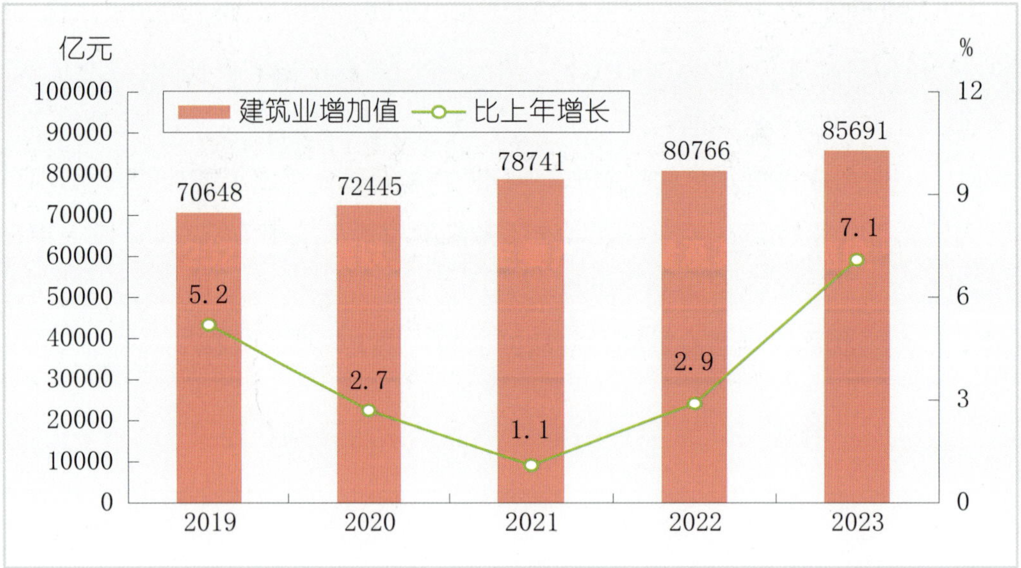

四、服务业

全年批发和零售业增加值123072亿元，比上年增长6.2%；交通运输、仓储和邮政业增加值57820亿元，增长8.0%；住宿和餐饮业增加值21024亿元，增长14.5%；金融业增加值100677亿元，增长6.8%；房地产业增加值73723亿元，下降1.3%；信息传输、软件和信息技术服务业增加值55194亿元，增长11.9%；租赁和商务服务业增加值44347亿元，增长9.3%。规模以上服务业企业营业收入比上年增长8.3%，利润总额增长26.8%。

图 11 2019-2023 年服务业增加值及其增长速度

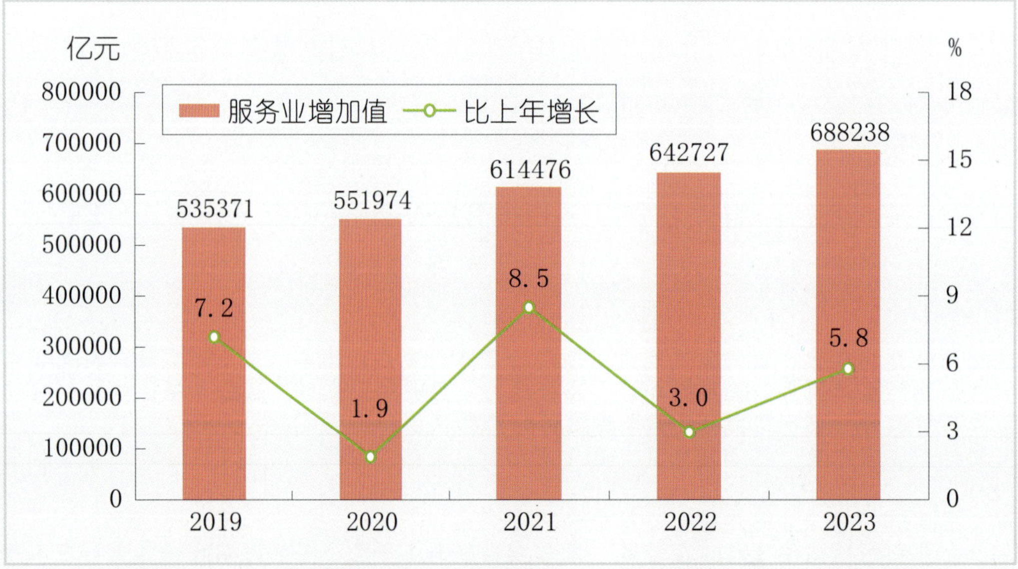

全年货物运输总量[28]557亿吨，比上年增长8.1%。货物运输周转量247713亿吨公里，增长6.3%。港口完成货物吞吐量170亿吨，比上年增长8.2%，其中外贸货物吞吐量50亿吨，增长9.5%。港口集装箱吞吐量31034万标准箱，增长4.9%。

表 5 2023 年各种运输方式完成货物运输量及其增长速度

指 标	单 位	绝对数	比上年增长（%）
货物运输总量	**亿吨**	**556.8**	**8.1**
铁路	亿吨	50.1	1.5
公路	亿吨	403.4	8.7
水路	亿吨	93.7	9.5
民航	万吨	735.4	21.0
管道	亿吨	9.5	7.5
货物运输周转量	**亿吨公里**	**247712.7**	**6.3**
铁路	亿吨公里	36437.6	1.5
公路	亿吨公里	73950.2	6.9
水路	亿吨公里	129951.5	7.4
民航	亿吨公里	283.6	11.6
管道	亿吨公里	7089.8	3.8

全年旅客运输总量93亿人次，比上年增长66.5%。旅客运输周转量28610亿人公里，增长121.4%。

表 6 2023 年各种运输方式完成旅客运输量及其增长速度

指 标	单 位	绝对数	比上年增长（%）
旅客运输总量	**亿人次**	**93.0**	**66.5**
铁路	亿人次	38.5	130.4
公路	亿人次	45.7	28.9
水路	亿人次	2.6	121.6
民航	亿人次	6.2	146.1
旅客运输周转量	**亿人公里**	**28609.6**	**121.4**
铁路	亿人公里	14729.4	123.9
公路	亿人公里	3517.6	46.1
水路	亿人公里	53.8	137.9
民航	亿人公里	10308.8	163.4

年末全国民用汽车保有量33618万辆（包括三轮汽车和低速货车706万辆），比上年末增加1714万辆，其中私人汽车保有量29427万辆，增加1553万辆。民用轿车保有量18668万辆，增加928万辆，其中私人轿车保有量17541万辆，增加856万辆。

[28] 货物运输总量及周转量包括铁路、公路、水路、民航和管道五种运输方式完成量，2023 年增速按可比口径计算。

全年完成邮政行业寄递业务总量[29]1625亿件，比上年增长16.8%。邮政业完成邮政函件业务9.7亿件，包裹业务0.2亿件，快递业务量1320.7亿件，快递业务收入12074亿元。全年完成电信业务总量[30]18327亿元，比上年增长16.8%。年末移动电话基站数[31]1162万个，其中4G基站629万个，5G基站338万个。全国电话用户总数189992万户，其中移动电话用户172660万户。移动电话普及率为122.5部/百人。固定互联网宽带接入用户[32]63631万户，比上年末增加4666万户，其中100M速率及以上的宽带接入用户[33]60136万户，增加4756万户。蜂窝物联网终端用户[34]23.32亿户，增加4.88亿户。互联网上网人数10.92亿人，其中手机上网人数10.91亿人。互联网普及率为77.5%，其中农村地区互联网普及率为66.5%。全年移动互联网用户接入流量3015亿GB，比上年增长15.2%。软件和信息技术服务业[35]完成软件业务收入123258亿元，比上年增长13.4%。

图12 2019-2023年快递业务量及其增长速度

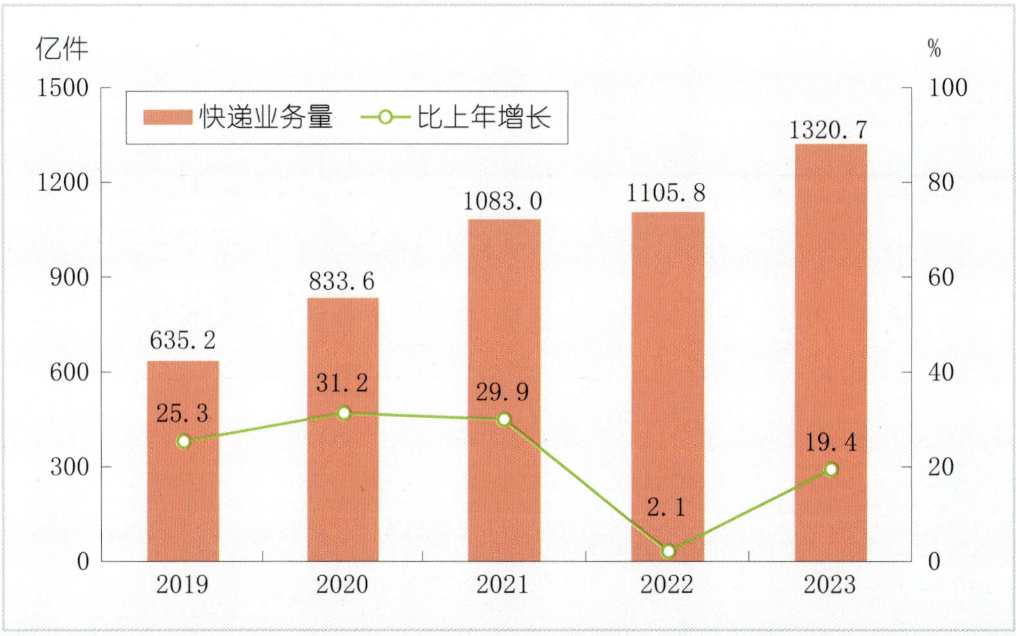

[29] 邮政行业寄递业务总量是指企业从事各类邮政普遍服务业务、快递业务的总数量。
[30] 电信业务总量按上年价格计算。
[31] 移动电话基站数是指报告期末为小区服务的无线收发信设备，处理基站与移动台之间的无线通信，在移动交换机与移动台之间起中继作用，监视无线传输质量的全套设备数。
[32] 固定互联网宽带接入用户是指报告期末在电信企业登记注册，通过xDSL、FTTx+LAN、FTTH/O以及其他宽带接入方式和普通专线接入公众互联网的用户。
[33] 100M速率及以上的宽带接入用户是指报告期末下行速率大于或等于100Mbit/s的宽带接入用户。
[34] 蜂窝物联网终端用户是指报告期末接入移动通信网络并开通物联网业务的用户。物联网终端即连接传感网络层和传输网络层，实现远程采集数据及向网络层发送数据的物联网设备。
[35] 软件和信息技术服务业包括软件开发、集成电路设计、信息系统集成和物联网技术服务、运行维护服务、信息处理和存储支持服务、信息技术咨询服务、数字内容服务和其他信息技术服务等行业。2023年软件和信息技术服务业完成软件业务收入增速按可比口径计算。

图 13　2019-2023 年年末固定互联网宽带接入用户数

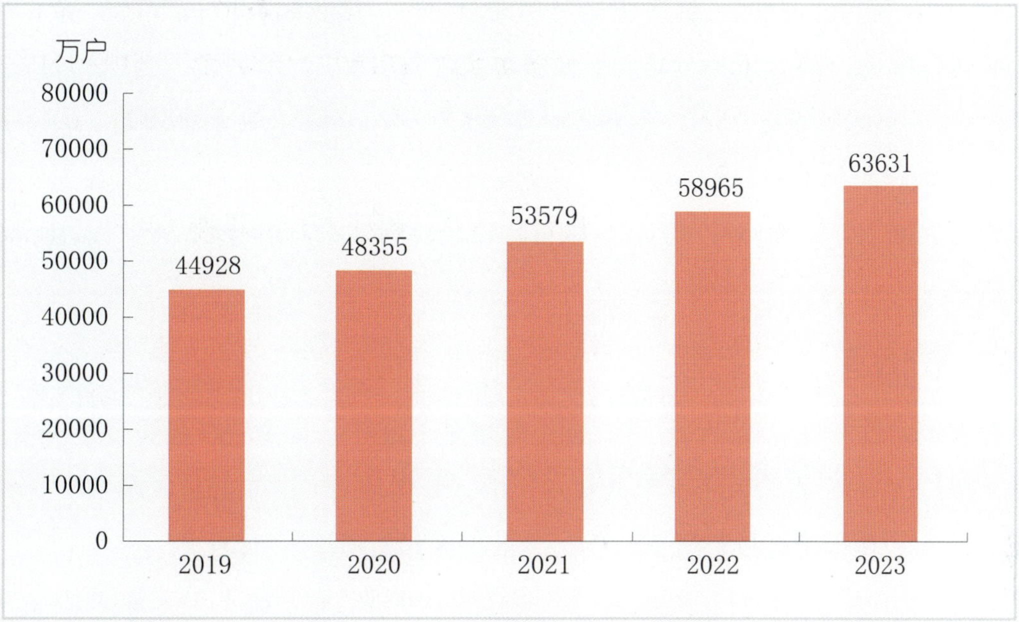

五、国内贸易

全年社会消费品零售总额471495亿元，比上年增长7.2%。按经营地分，城镇消费品零售额407490亿元，增长7.1%；乡村消费品零售额64005亿元，增长8.0%。按消费类型分，商品零售额418605亿元，增长5.8%；餐饮收入52890亿元，增长20.4%。服务零售额[36]比上年增长20.0%。

图 14　2019-2023 年社会消费品零售总额及其增长速度

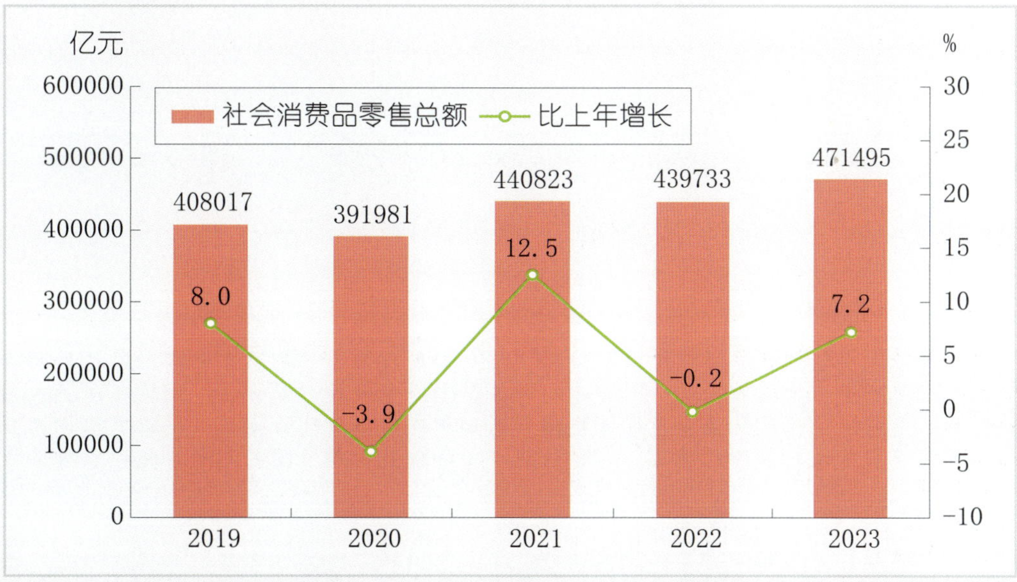

[36] 服务零售额是指企业（产业活动单位、个体户）以交易形式直接提供给个人和其他单位非生产、非经营用的服务价值总和，旨在反映服务提供方以货币形式销售的属于消费的服务价值，包括交通、住宿、餐饮、教育、卫生、体育、娱乐等领域服务活动的零售额。

全年限额以上单位商品零售额中，粮油、食品类零售额比上年增长5.2%，饮料类增长3.2%，烟酒类增长10.6%，服装、鞋帽、针纺织品类增长12.9%，化妆品类增长5.1%，金银珠宝类增长13.3%，日用品类增长2.7%，家用电器和音像器材类增长0.5%，中西药品类增长5.1%，文化办公用品类下降6.1%，家具类增长2.8%，通讯器材类增长7.0%，石油及制品类增长6.6%，汽车类增长5.9%，建筑及装潢材料类下降7.8%。

全年实物商品网上零售额130174亿元，按可比口径计算，比上年增长8.4%，占社会消费品零售总额比重为27.6%。

六、固定资产投资

全年全社会固定资产投资509708亿元，比上年增长[37]2.8%。固定资产投资（不含农户）503036亿元，增长3.0%。在固定资产投资（不含农户）中，分区域看[38]，东部地区投资增长4.4%，中部地区投资增长0.3%，西部地区投资增长0.1%，东北地区投资下降1.8%。

在固定资产投资（不含农户）中，第一产业投资10085亿元，比上年下降0.1%；第二产业投资162136亿元，增长9.0%；第三产业投资330815亿元，增长0.4%。基础设施投资[39]增长5.9%。社会领域投资[40]增长0.5%。民间固定资产投资[41]253544亿元，下降0.4%；其中制造业民间投资增长9.4%，基础设施民间投资增长14.2%。

---

[37] 固定资产投资相关指标增速按可比口径计算。报告期数据与上年已公布的同期数据之间存在不可比因素，不能直接相比计算增速。主要原因是：①改进和完善数据质量审核评估方法，剔除不应纳入报告期完成投资的前期土地费用以及跨地区、跨行业重复统计数据。②加强在建投资项目审核，剔除流动资产、消耗性生物资产等不符合固定资产投资统计范围的项目。③加强统计执法检查，对发现的问题数据按照相关规定进行了改正。

[38] 见注释[20]。

[39] 基础设施投资包括铁路运输业、道路运输业、水上运输业、航空运输业、管道运输业、多式联运和运输代理业、装卸搬运业、邮政业、电信广播电视和卫星传输服务业、互联网和相关服务业、水利管理业、生态保护和环境治理业、公共设施管理业投资。

[40] 社会领域投资包括教育，卫生和社会工作，文化、体育和娱乐业投资。

[41] 民间固定资产投资是指具有集体、私营、个人性质的内资企事业单位以及由其控股（包括绝对控股和相对控股）的企业单位建造或购置固定资产的投资。

图 15　2023 年三次产业投资占固定资产投资（不含农户）比重

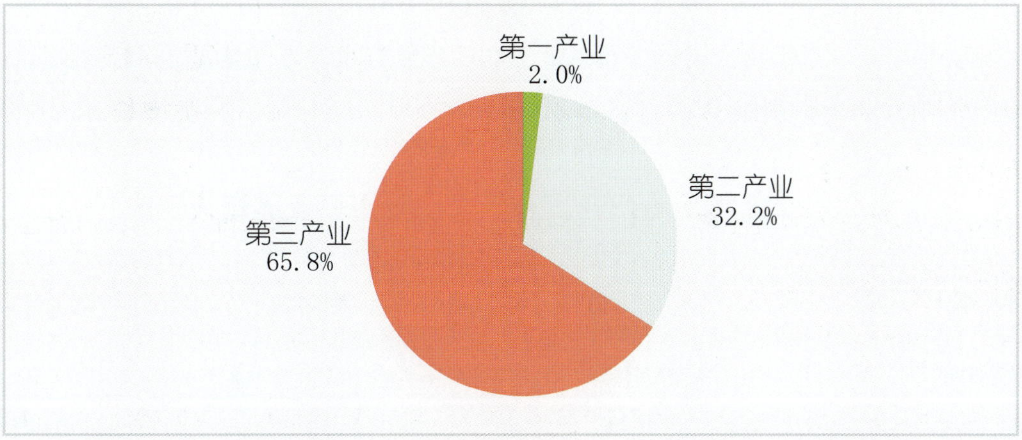

表 7　2023 年分行业固定资产投资（不含农户）增长速度

行　业	比上年增长（%）	行　业	比上年增长（%）
总　计	3.0	金融业	-11.9
农、林、牧、渔业	1.2	房地产业[42]	-8.1
采矿业	2.1	租赁和商务服务业	9.9
制造业	6.5	科学研究和技术服务业	18.1
电力、热力、燃气及水生产和供应业	23.0	水利、环境和公共设施管理业	0.1
建筑业	22.5	居民服务、修理和其他服务业	15.8
批发和零售业	-0.4	教育	2.8
交通运输、仓储和邮政业	10.5	卫生和社会工作	-3.8
住宿和餐饮业	8.2	文化、体育和娱乐业	2.6
信息传输、软件和信息技术服务业	13.8	公共管理、社会保障和社会组织	-37.0

表 8　2023 年固定资产投资新增主要生产与运营能力

指　标	单　位	绝对数
新增 220 千伏及以上交流变电设备容量	万千伏安	25656
新建铁路投产里程	公里	3637
其中：高速铁路	公里	2776
增、新建铁路复线投产里程	公里	3351
电气化铁路投产里程	公里	4463
新改建高速公路里程	公里	7498
港口万吨级及以上码头泊位新增通过能力	万吨/年	32529
新增民用运输机场	个	5
新增光缆线路长度	万公里	474

[42] 房地产业投资除房地产开发投资外，还包括建设单位自建房屋以及物业管理、中介服务和其他房地产投资。

全年房地产开发投资110913亿元，比上年下降[43]9.6%。其中住宅投资83820亿元，下降9.3%；办公楼投资4531亿元，下降9.4%；商业营业用房投资8055亿元，下降16.9%。全年新建商品房销售面积[44]111735万平方米。二手房交易网签面积[45]70882万平方米。年末新建商品房待售面积67295万平方米，其中商品住宅待售面积33119万平方米。

表9 2023年房地产开发和销售主要指标及其增长速度

指 标	单 位	绝对数	比上年增长（%）
房地产开发投资	亿元	110913	-9.6
其中：住宅	亿元	83820	-9.3
房屋施工面积	万平方米	838364	-7.2
其中：住宅	万平方米	589884	-7.7
房屋新开工面积	万平方米	95376	-20.4
其中：住宅	万平方米	69286	-20.9
房屋竣工面积	万平方米	99831	17.0
其中：住宅	万平方米	72433	17.2
新建商品房销售面积	万平方米	111735	-8.5
其中：住宅	万平方米	94796	-8.2
房地产开发企业本年到位资金	亿元	127459	-13.6
其中：国内贷款	亿元	15595	-9.9
个人按揭贷款	亿元	21489	-9.1

全年全国各类棚户区改造开工159万套，基本建成193万套；保障性租赁住房开工建设和筹集213万套（间）。新开工改造城镇老旧小区5.37万个，涉及居民897万户。

七、对外经济

全年货物进出口总额417568亿元，比上年增长0.2%。其中，出口237726亿元，增长0.6%；进口179842亿元，下降0.3%。货物进出口顺差57883亿元，比上年增加1938亿元。对共建“一带一路”[46]国家进出口额194719亿元，比上年增长2.8%。其中，出口107314亿元，增长6.9%；进口

[43] 房地产开发投资和新建商品房销售等指标增速按可比口径计算。报告期数据与上年已公布的同期数据之间存在不可比因素，不能直接相比计算增速。主要原因是：①加强在建房地产开发项目审核，剔除单纯一级土地开发等非房地产开发项目。②加强商品房销售数据审核，剔除退房和具有抵押性质等非商品房销售数据。③加强统计执法，对发现的问题数据按照相关规定进行了改正。

[44] 新建商品房销售面积是指报告期内房地产开发企业出售的新建商品房屋的合同总面积。

[45] 二手房交易网签面积是指报告期内城镇二手房网签交易合同总面积。

[46] “一带一路”是指“丝绸之路经济带”和“21世纪海上丝绸之路”。

87405亿元，下降1.9%。对《区域全面经济伙伴关系协定》（RCEP）其他成员国[47]进出口额125967亿元，比上年下降1.6%。民营企业进出口额223601亿元，比上年增长6.3%，占进出口总额比重为53.5%。

图16 2019-2023年货物进出口总额

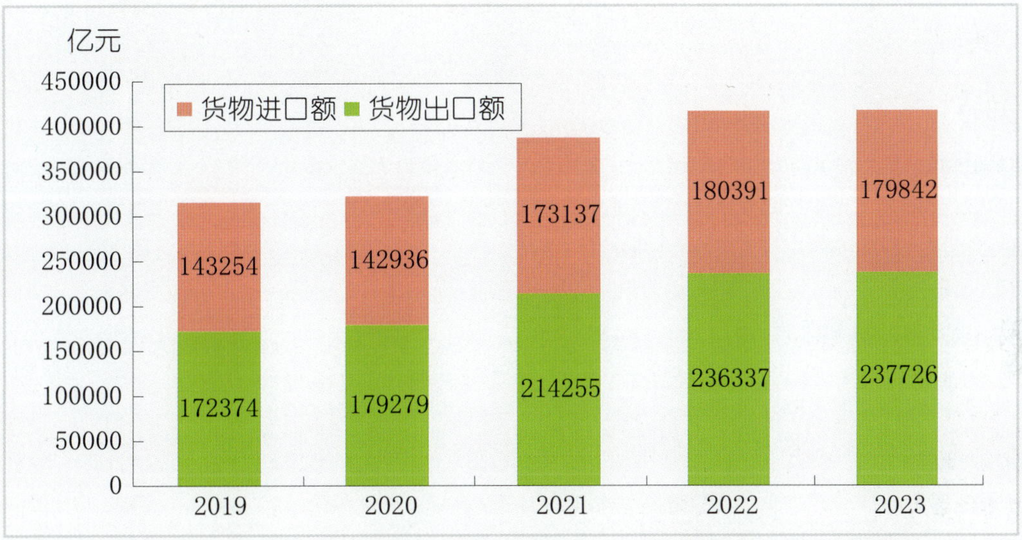

表10 2023年货物进出口总额及其增长速度

指 标	金额（亿元）	比上年增长（%）
货物进出口总额	**417568**	**0.2**
货物出口额	237726	0.6
其中：一般贸易	153530	2.5
加工贸易	49062	-9.0
其中：机电产品	139196	2.9
高新技术产品	59279	-5.8
货物进口额	179842	-0.3
其中：一般贸易	117042	1.3
加工贸易	27061	-11.3
其中：机电产品	65363	-5.5
高新技术产品	47916	-5.2
货物进出口顺差	**57883**	**3.5**

[47]《区域全面经济伙伴关系协定》(RCEP)其他成员国包括印度尼西亚、马来西亚、菲律宾、泰国、新加坡、文莱、柬埔寨、老挝、缅甸、越南、日本、韩国、澳大利亚、新西兰。

表11 2023年主要商品出口数量、金额及其增长速度

商品名称	单位	数量	比上年增长（%）	金额（亿元）	比上年增长（%）
钢材	万吨	9026	36.2	5929	-3.4
纺织纱线、织物及其制品	—	—	—	9454	-3.1
服装及衣着附件	—	—	—	11206	-2.8
鞋靴	万双	891424	-2.5	3470	-8.0
家具及其零件	—	—	—	4517	0.2
箱包及类似容器	万吨	331	13.5	2512	9.3
玩具	—	—	—	2858	-7.4
塑料制品	—	—	—	7090	1.4
集成电路	亿个	2678	-1.8	9568	-5.0
自动数据处理设备及其零部件	—	—	—	13187	-15.8
手机	万台	80213	-2.0	9797	2.9
集装箱	万个	231	-27.9	581	-39.8
液晶平板显示模组	万个	168929	2.9	1873	3.8
汽车（包括底盘）	万辆	522	57.4	7165	76.8

表12 2023年主要商品进口数量、金额及其增长速度

商品名称	单位	数量	比上年增长（%）	金额（亿元）	比上年增长（%）
大豆	万吨	9941	11.4	4199	4.8
食用植物油	万吨	981	51.4	734	21.1
铁矿砂及其精矿	万吨	117906	6.6	9418	11.2
煤及褐煤	万吨	47442	61.8	3723	30.2
原油	万吨	56399	11.0	23733	-2.6
成品油	万吨	4769	80.3	1965	50.0
天然气	万吨	11997	9.9	4523	-3.4
初级形状的塑料	万吨	2960	-3.2	3182	-14.8
纸浆	万吨	3666	25.7	1665	11.6
钢材	万吨	765	-27.6	891	-21.5
未锻轧铜及铜材	万吨	550	-6.3	3356	-6.9
集成电路	亿个	4796	-10.8	24591	-10.6
汽车（包括底盘）	万辆	80	-8.9	3321	-5.8

表 13 2023 年对主要国家和地区货物进出口金额、增长速度及其比重

国家和地区	出口额（亿元）	比上年增长（%）	占全部出口比重（%）	进口额（亿元）	比上年增长（%）	占全部进口比重（%）
东盟	36817	0.0	15.5	27309	0.4	15.2
欧盟	35226	-5.3	14.8	19833	4.6	11.0
美国	35198	-8.1	14.8	11528	-1.8	6.4
日本	11076	-3.5	4.7	11309	-7.9	6.3
韩国	10467	-2.2	4.4	11381	-13.9	6.3
中国香港	19333	-1.3	8.1	958	84.3	0.5
中国台湾	4819	-11.1	2.0	14033	-10.5	7.8
俄罗斯	7823	53.9	3.3	9093	18.6	5.1
巴西	4159	1.0	1.7	8625	18.4	4.8
印度	8279	6.5	3.5	1301	12.2	0.7
南非	1661	4.4	0.7	2245	3.7	1.2

全年服务进出口总额65754亿元，比上年增长10.0%。其中，出口26857亿元，下降5.8%；进口38898亿元，增长24.4%。服务进出口逆差12041亿元。

全年外商直接投资新设立企业53766家，比上年增长39.7%。实际使用外商直接投资额11339亿元，下降8.0%，折1633亿美元，下降13.7%。其中，共建“一带一路”国家对华直接投资（含通过部分自由港对华投资）新设立企业13649家，增长82.7%；对华直接投资额1221亿元，下降11.4%，折176亿美元，下降16.7%。高技术产业实际使用外资额4233亿元，下降4.9%，折610亿美元，下降10.8%。

表 14 2023 年外商直接投资额及其增长速度

行 业	企业数（家）	比上年增长（%）	实际使用金额（亿元）	比上年增长（%）
总 计	53766	39.7	11339	-8.0
其中：农、林、牧、渔业	418	-0.5	51	-36.8
制造业	3624	1.5	3179	-1.8
电力、热力、燃气及水生产和供应业	568	8.6	319	15.6
交通运输、仓储和邮政业	867	44.0	149	-57.2
信息传输、软件和信息技术服务业	3764	23.0	1134	-26.7
批发和零售业	18010	65.3	690	-28.2
房地产业	684	17.7	810	-11.4
租赁和商务服务业	10673	42.8	1819	-15.4
居民服务、修理和其他服务业	726	76.6	34	77.7

全年对外非金融类直接投资额9170亿元，比上年增长16.7%，折1301亿美元，增长11.4%。其中，对共建“一带一路”国家非金融类直接投资额2241亿元，增长28.4%，折318亿美元，增长22.6%。

表15 2023年对外非金融类直接投资额及其增长速度

行　业	金额（亿美元）	比上年增长（%）
总　计	1301	11.4
其中：农、林、牧、渔业	8	-3.6
采矿业	70	39.0
制造业	279	29.0
电力、热力、燃气及水生产和供应业	31	-12.5
建筑业	67	5.1
批发和零售业	292	38.6
交通运输、仓储和邮政业	65	42.3
信息传输、软件和信息技术服务业	49	-10.9
房地产业	10	-57.4
租赁和商务服务业	337	-13.0

全年对外承包工程完成营业额11339亿元，比上年增长8.8%，折1609亿美元，增长3.8%。其中，对共建“一带一路”国家完成营业额1321亿美元，增长4.8%，占对外承包工程完成营业额比重为82.1%。对外劳务合作派出各类劳务人员35万人。

八、财政金融

全年全国一般公共预算收入216784亿元，比上年增长6.4%；其中税收收入181129亿元，增长8.7%。全国一般公共预算支出274574亿元，比上年增长5.4%。全年新增减税降费及退税缓费超2.2万亿元。

图17 2019-2023年全国一般公共预算收入

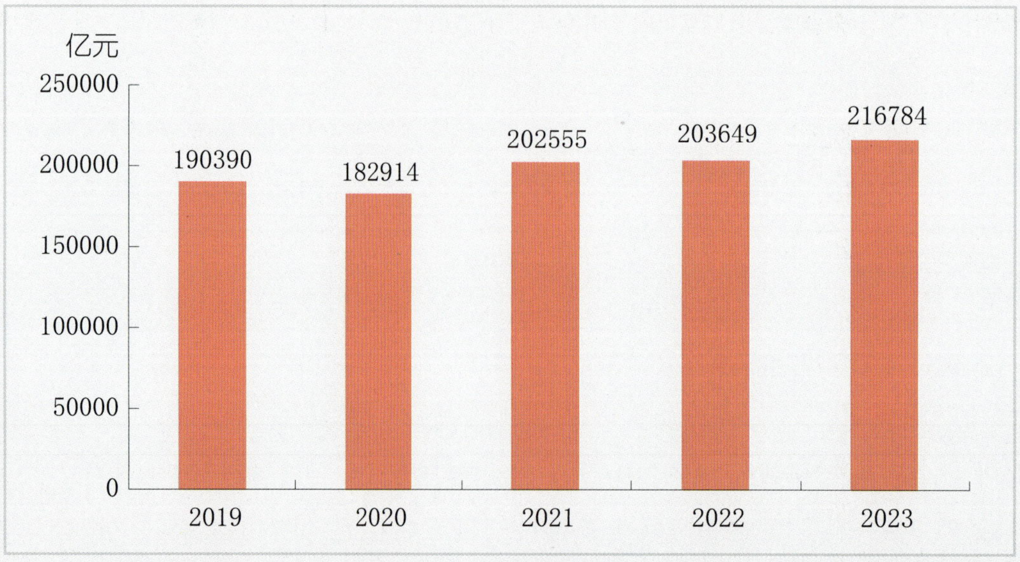

注：图中2019年至2022年数据为全国一般公共预算收入决算数，2023年为执行数。

年末广义货币供应量（M_2）余额292.3万亿元，比上年末增长9.7%；狭义货币供应量（M_1）余额68.1万亿元，增长1.3%；流通中货币（M_0）余额11.3万亿元，增长8.3%。

全年社会融资规模增量[48]35.6万亿元，按可比口径计算，比上年多3.4万亿元。年末社会融资规模存量[49]378.1万亿元，按可比口径计算，比上年末增长9.5%，其中对实体经济发放的人民币贷款余额235.5万亿元，增长10.4%。年末全部金融机构本外币各项存款余额289.9万亿元，比年初增加25.4万亿元，其中人民币各项存款余额284.3万亿元，增加25.7万亿元。全部金融机构本外币各项贷款余额242.2万亿元，增加22.2万亿元，其中人民币各项贷款余额237.6万亿元，增加22.7万亿元。人民币普惠小微贷款[50]余额29.4万亿元，增加5.6万亿元。人民币制造业中长期贷款余额12.2万亿元，增加3.1万亿元。

表 16　2023 年年末全部金融机构本外币存贷款余额及其增长速度

指　标	年末数（亿元）	比上年末增长（%）
各项存款	**2899132**	**9.6**
其中：境内住户存款	1378765	13.8
其中：人民币	1369895	13.8
境内非金融企业存款	817959	4.9
各项贷款	**2422396**	**10.1**
其中：境内短期贷款	623037	10.2
境内中长期贷款	1591965	11.3

年末主要农村金融机构（农村信用社、农村合作银行、农村商业银行）人民币贷款余额293584亿元，比年初增加26363亿元。全部金融机构人民币消费贷款余额579438亿元，增加10992亿元。其中，住户短期消费贷款余额103541亿元，增加5078亿元；住户中长期消费贷款余额475897亿元，增加5914亿元。

全年沪深交易所A股累计筹资[51]10734亿元，比上年减少4375亿元。沪深交易所首次公开发行上市A股236只，筹资3418亿元，比上年减少2286亿元，其中科创板股票67只，筹资1439亿元；沪深交易所A股再融资（包括公开增发、定向增发、配股、优先股、可转债转股）7316亿元，减少2089亿

[48] 社会融资规模增量是指一定时期内实体经济从金融体系获得的资金总额。
[49] 社会融资规模存量是指一定时期末（月末、季末或年末）实体经济从金融体系获得的资金余额。
[50] 普惠小微贷款包括单户授信小于 1000 万元的小微型企业贷款、个体工商户经营性贷款、小微企业主经营性贷款。
[51] 沪深交易所股票筹资额按上市日统计，筹资额包括了可转债实际转股金额，2022 年、2023 年可转债实际转股金额分别为 934 亿元、832 亿元。

元。北京证券交易所公开发行股票77只，筹资[52]146亿元。全年各类主体通过沪深北交易所发行债券（包括公司债券、资产支持证券、国债、地方政府债券和政策性银行债券）筹资130677亿元，其中沪深交易所共发行上市基础设施领域不动产投资信托基金（REITs）40只，募集资金914亿元。全国中小企业股份转让系统[53]挂牌公司6241家，全年挂牌公司累计股票筹资180亿元。

全年发行公司信用类债券[54]13.8万亿元，比上年增加0.1万亿元。

全年保险公司原保险保费收入[55]51247亿元，比上年增长9.1%。其中，寿险业务原保险保费收入27646亿元，健康险和意外伤害险业务原保险保费收入9993亿元，财产险业务原保险保费收入13607亿元。支付各类赔款及给付18883亿元。其中，寿险业务给付5505亿元，健康险和意外伤害险业务赔款及给付4207亿元，财产险业务赔款9171亿元。

九、居民收入消费和社会保障

全年全国居民人均可支配收入39218元，比上年增长6.3%，扣除价格因素，实际增长6.1%。全国居民人均可支配收入中位数[56]33036元，增长5.3%。按常住地分，城镇居民人均可支配收入51821元，比上年增长5.1%，扣除价格因素，实际增长4.8%。城镇居民人均可支配收入中位数47122元，增长4.4%。农村居民人均可支配收入21691元，比上年增长7.7%，扣除价格因素，实际增长7.6%。农村居民人均可支配收入中位数18748元，增长5.7%。城乡居民人均可支配收入比值为2.39，比上年缩小0.06。按全国居民五等份收入分组[57]，低收入组人均可支配收入9215元，中间偏下收入组人均可支配收入20442元，中间收入组人均可支配收入32195元，中间偏上收入组人均可支配收入50220元，高收入组人均可支配收入95055元。全国农民工人均月收入4780元，比上年增长3.6%。脱贫县[58]农村居民人均可支配收入16396元，比上年增长8.5%，扣除价格因素，实际增长8.4%。

全年全国居民人均消费支出26796元，比上年增长9.2%，扣除价格因素，实际增长9.0%。其中，人均服务性消费支出[59]12114元，比上年增长14.4%，占居民人均消费支出比重为45.2%。按常住地分，城镇居民人均消费支出32994元，增长8.6%，扣除价格因素，实际增长8.3%；农村居民人

[52] 北京证券交易所股票筹资额按上市日统计。

[53] 全国中小企业股份转让系统是2012年经国务院批准的全国性证券交易场所。全年全国中小企业股份转让系统挂牌公司累计筹资不含优先股，股票筹资按新增股份挂牌日统计。

[54] 公司信用类债券包括非金融企业债务融资工具、企业债券以及公司债、可转债等。

[55] 原保险保费收入是指保险企业确认的原保险合同保费收入。

[56] 人均可支配收入中位数是指将所有调查户按人均收入水平从低到高（或从高到低）顺序排列，处于最中间位置调查户的人均可支配收入。

[57] 全国居民五等份收入分组是指将所有调查户按人均收入水平从低到高顺序排列，平均分为五个等份，处于最低20%的收入家庭为低收入组，依此类推依次为中间偏下收入组、中间收入组、中间偏上收入组、高收入组。

[58] 脱贫县包括原832个国家扶贫开发工作重点县和集中连片特困地区县，以及新疆阿克苏地区7个市县。

[59] 服务性消费支出是指住户用于各种生活服务的消费支出，包括餐饮服务、衣着鞋类加工服务、居住服务、家庭服务、交通通信服务、教育文化娱乐服务、医疗服务和其他服务。

均消费支出18175元，增长9.3%，扣除价格因素，实际增长9.2%。全国居民恩格尔系数为29.8%，其中城镇为28.8%，农村为32.4%。

图 18 2019-2023 年全国居民人均可支配收入及其增长速度

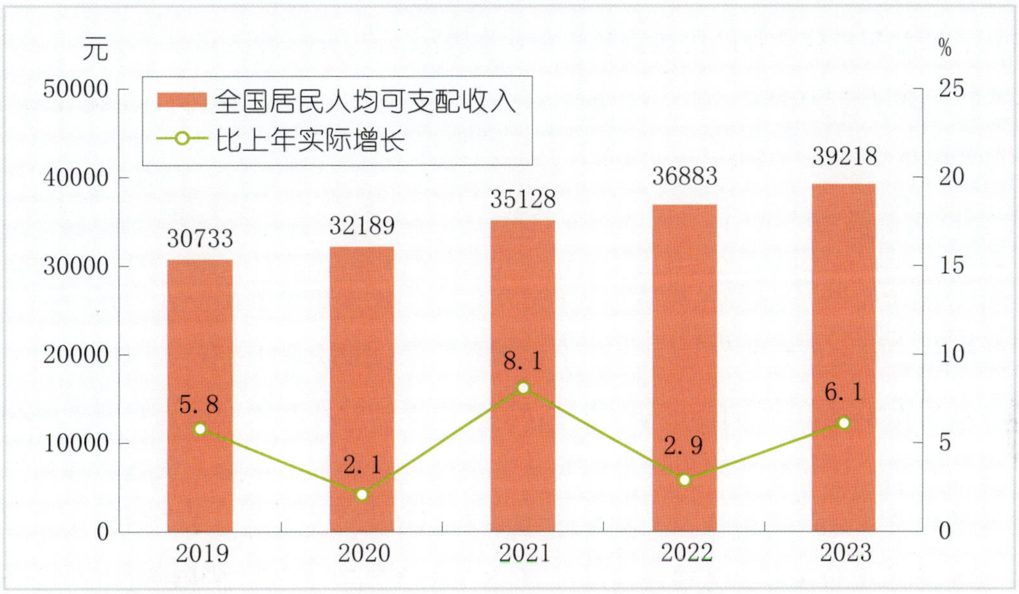

图 19 2023 年全国居民人均消费支出及其构成

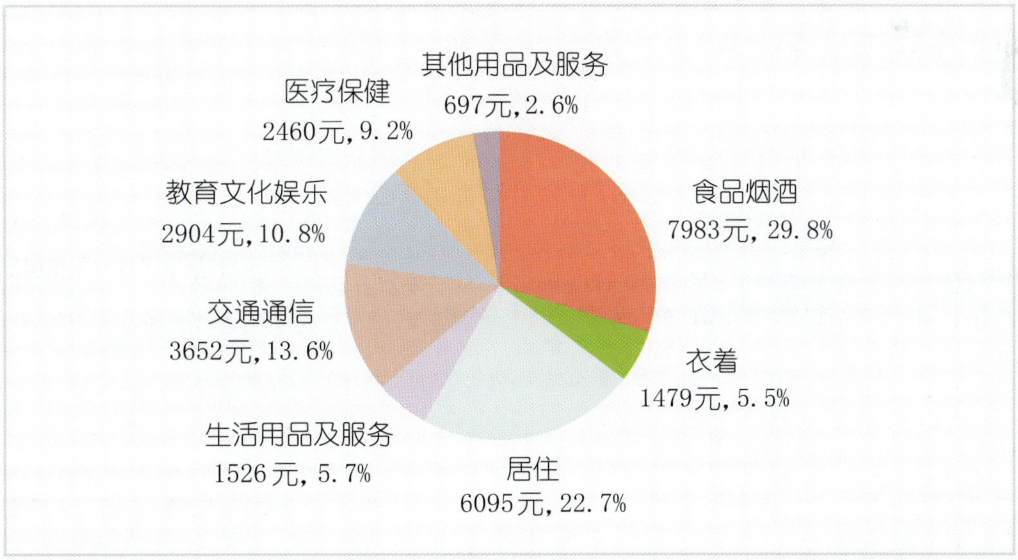

年末全国参加城镇职工基本养老保险人数52121万人，比上年末增加1766万人。参加城乡居民基本养老保险人数54522万人，减少430万人。参加基本医疗保险人数[60]133387万人，其中参加职工基本医疗保险人数37094万人，参加城乡居民基本医疗保险人数96293万人。参加失业保险人数

[60] 2023 年基本医疗保险参保人数剔除部分重复参保情况。

24373万人，增加566万人。领取失业保险金人数352万人。参加工伤保险人数30170万人，增加1054万人。参加生育保险人数24907万人。年末全国共有664万人享受城市最低生活保障，3399万人享受农村最低生活保障，435万人享受农村特困人员[61]救助供养，全年临时救助[62]742万人次。全年领取国家定期抚恤金、定期生活补助金的退役军人和其他优抚对象834万人。

年末全国共有各类提供住宿的民政服务机构4.4万个，其中养老机构4.1万个，儿童福利和救助保护机构971个。民政服务床位[63]846.3万张，其中养老服务床位820.1万张，儿童福利和救助保护机构床位9.8万张。

十、科学技术和教育

全年研究与试验发展（R&D）经费支出33278亿元，比上年增长8.1%，与国内生产总值之比为2.64%，其中基础研究经费2212亿元，比上年增长9.3%，占R&D经费支出比重为6.65%。国家自然科学基金共资助5.25万个项目。截至年末，纳入新序列管理的国家工程研究中心207个，国家企业技术中心1798家。国家科技成果转化引导基金累计设立36只子基金，资金总规模624亿元。国家级科技企业孵化器[64]1606家，国家备案众创空间[65]2376家。全年授予发明专利权92.1万件，比上年增长15.3%。PCT专利申请受理量[66]7.4万件。截至年末，有效发明专利499.1万件，比上年末增长18.5%。每万人口高价值发明专利拥有量[67]11.8件。全年商标注册438.3万件，比上年下降29.0%。全年共签订技术合同95万项，技术合同成交金额61476亿元，比上年增长28.6%。我国公民具备科学素质[68]的比例达到14.14%。

---

[61] 农村特困人员是指无劳动能力，无生活来源，无法定赡养、抚养、扶养义务人或者其法定义务人无履行义务能力的农村老年人、残疾人以及未满16周岁的未成年人。

[62] 临时救助是指国家对遭遇突发事件、意外伤害、重大疾病或其他特殊原因导致基本生活陷入困境，其他社会救助制度暂时无法覆盖或救助之后基本生活暂时仍有严重困难的家庭或个人给予的应急性、过渡性的救助。

[63] 民政服务床位除收养性机构外，还包括救助类机构、社区类机构的床位。

[64] 国家级科技企业孵化器是指符合《科技企业孵化器管理办法》规定的，以促进科技成果转化、培育科技企业和企业家精神为宗旨，提供物理空间、共享设施和专业化服务的科技创业服务机构，且经过科学技术部批准确定的科技企业孵化器。

[65] 国家备案众创空间是指符合《发展众创空间工作指引》规定的新型创新创业服务平台，且按照《国家众创空间备案暂行规定》经科学技术部审核备案的众创空间。

[66] PCT专利申请受理量是指国家知识产权局作为PCT专利申请受理局受理的PCT专利申请数量。PCT(Patent Cooperation Treaty)即专利合作条约，是专利领域的一项国际合作条约。

[67] 每万人口高价值发明专利拥有量是指每万人口本国居民拥有的经国家知识产权局授权的符合下列任一条件的有效发明专利数量：战略性新兴产业的发明专利；在海外有同族专利权的发明专利；维持年限超过10年的发明专利；实现较高质押融资金额的发明专利；获得国家科学技术奖、中国专利奖的发明专利。

[68] 公民具备科学素质是指崇尚科学精神，树立科学思想，掌握基本科学方法，了解必要科技知识，并具有应用其分析判断事物和解决实际问题的能力。公民具备科学素质比例数据是面向18—69岁公民开展抽样调查获得。

图 20 2019-2023 年研究与试验发展（R&D）经费支出及其增长速度

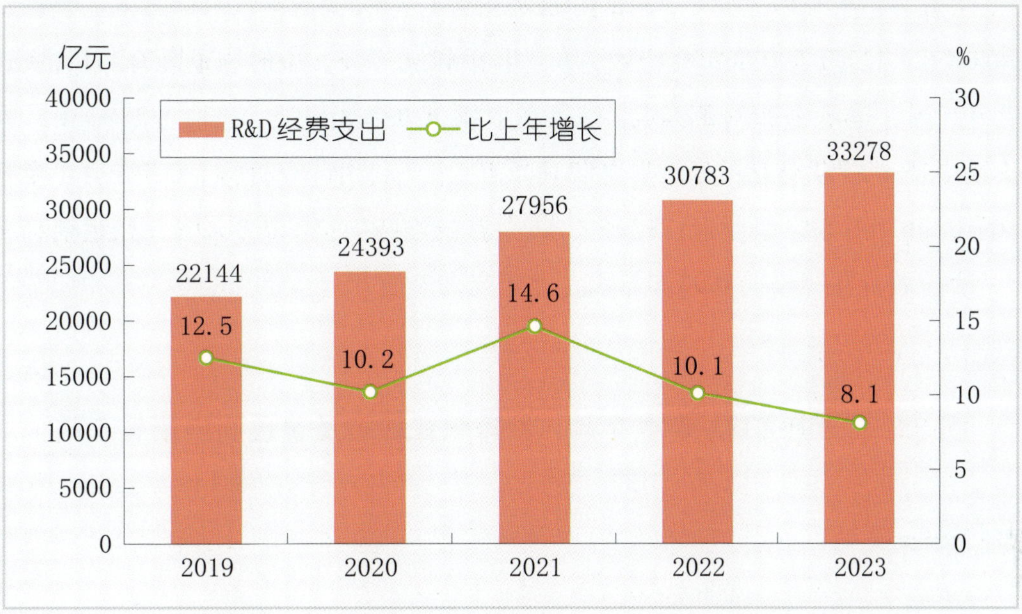

表 17 2023 年专利授权和有效专利情况

指　标	专利数（万件）	比上年增长（%）
发明专利授权	92.1	15.3
其中：境内发明专利授权	81.3	18.0
实用新型专利授权	209.0	-25.5
外观设计专利授权	63.8	-11.5
年末有效发明专利	499.1	18.5
其中：境内有效发明专利	401.5	22.4
年末有效实用新型专利	1212.9	11.9
年末有效外观设计专利	323.4	14.2

全年成功完成66次宇航发射。天舟六号、神舟十六号、神舟十七号任务相继实施，中国空间站进入应用与发展阶段。全球首枚液氧甲烷火箭朱雀二号遥二运载火箭成功发射。量子计算原型机九章三号成功构建。全超导托卡马克核聚变实验装置实现稳态高约束模式等离子体运行403秒。全球首座第四代核电站高温气冷堆示范工程投入商业运行。全球首台16兆瓦海上风电机组并网发电。C919大型客机正式投入商业运营。首艘国产大型邮轮完成试航。奋斗者号载人潜水器完成极限深潜。

年末全国共有国家质检中心877家。全国现有产品质量、体系和服务认证机构1242个，累计完成对102万家企业的认证。全年制定、修订国家标准2902项，其中新制定1708项。全年制造业产品质量合格率[69]为93.65%。

全年研究生教育招生130.2万人，在学研究生388.3万人，毕业生101.5万人。普通、职业本专科[70]招生1042.2万人，在校生3775.0万人，毕业生1047.0万人。中等职业教育[71]招生616.5万人，在校生1737.9万人，毕业生537.1万人。普通高中招生967.8万人，在校生2803.6万人，毕业生860.4万人。初中招生1754.6万人，在校生5243.7万人，毕业生1623.6万人。普通小学招生1877.9万人，在校生10836.0万人，毕业生1763.5万人。特殊教育招生15.5万人，在校生91.2万人，毕业生17.3万人。学前教育在园幼儿4093.0万人。九年义务教育巩固率为95.7%，高中阶段毛入学率为91.8%。

图21 2019-2023年本专科、中等职业教育及普通高中招生人数

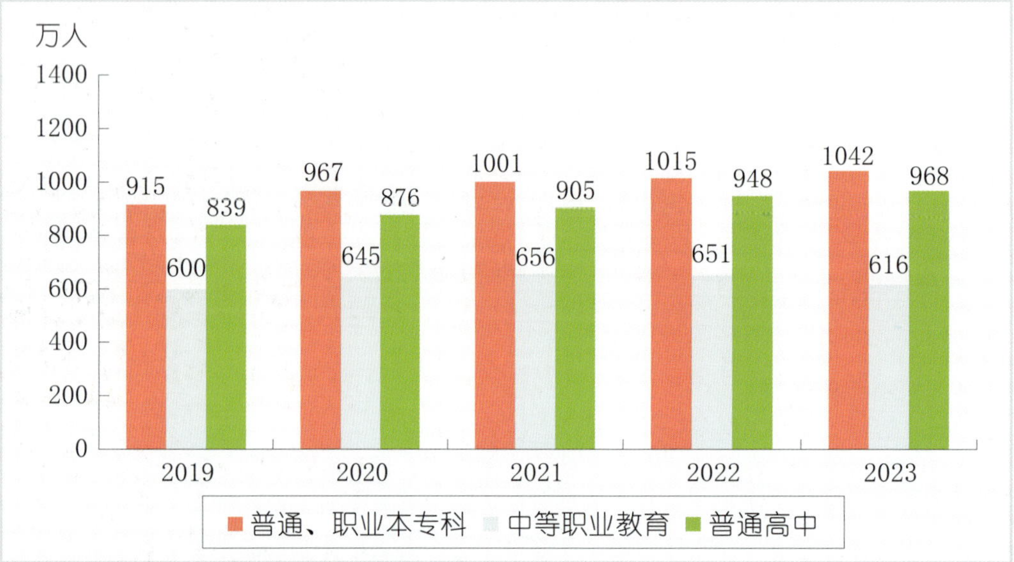

十一、文化旅游、卫生健康和体育

年末全国文化和旅游部门所属艺术表演团体1893个。全国共有公共图书馆3309个，总流通[72]112668万人次；文化馆3508个。有线电视实际用户2.02亿户，其中有线数字电视实际用户1.93亿户。年末广播节目综合人口覆盖率为99.7%，电视节目综合人口覆盖率为99.8%。全年生产电视剧156部4632集，

[69] 制造业产品质量合格率是指以产品质量检验为手段，按照规定的方法、程序和标准实施质量抽样检测，判定为质量合格的样品数占全部抽样样品数的百分比，统计调查样本覆盖制造业的29个行业。

[70] 普通、职业本专科包括普通本科、职业本科、高职（专科）。

[71] 中等职业教育包括普通中专、成人中专、职业高中和技工学校。

[72] 总流通人次是指本年度内到图书馆场馆接受图书馆服务的总人次，包括借阅书刊、咨询问题以及参加各类读者活动等。

电视动画片93811分钟。生产故事影片792部，科教、纪录、动画和特种影片[73]179部。出版各类报纸258亿份，各类期刊18亿册，图书119亿册（张），人均图书拥有量[74]8.40册（张）。年末全国共有档案馆4154个，已开放各类档案23827万卷（件）。全年全国规模以上文化及相关产业企业营业收入129515亿元，按可比口径计算，比上年增长8.2%。

全年国内出游48.9亿人次，比上年增长93.3%。其中，城镇居民国内出游37.6亿人次，增长94.9%；农村居民国内出游11.3亿人次，增长88.5%。国内游客出游总花费49133亿元，增长140.3%。其中，城镇居民出游花费41781亿元，增长147.5%；农村居民出游花费7353亿元，增长106.4%。入境游客8203万人次，其中外国人1378万人次，香港、澳门和台湾同胞6824万人次。入境游客总花费530亿美元。国内居民出境10096万人次，其中因私出境9684万人次，赴港澳台出境7704万人次。

图 22　2019-2023 年国内出游人次及其增长速度

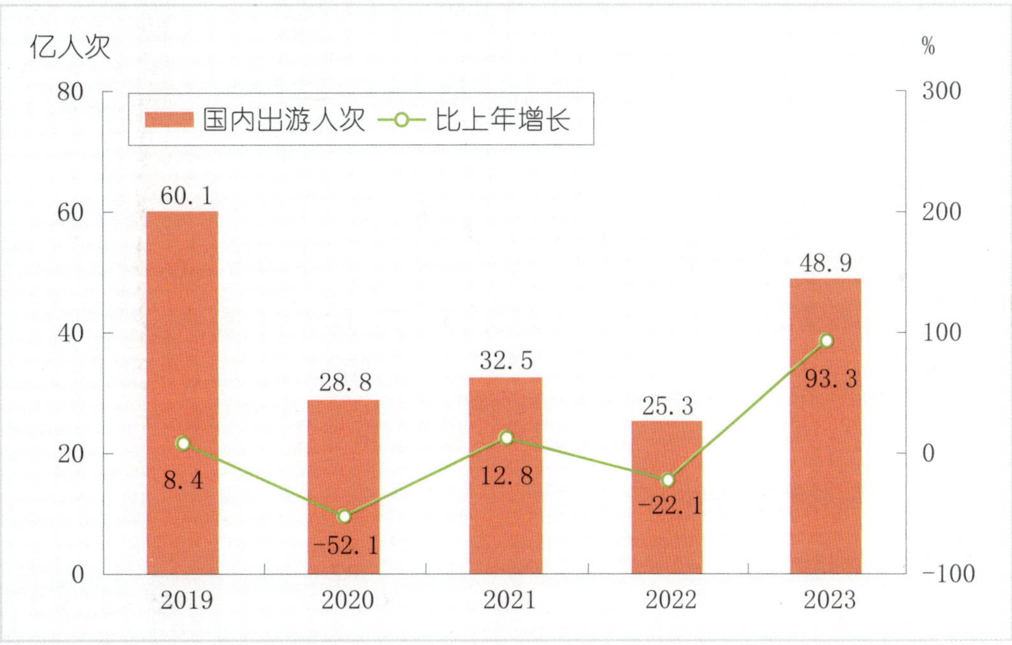

年末全国共有医疗卫生机构107.1万个，其中医院3.9万个，在医院中有公立医院1.2万个，民营医院2.7万个；基层医疗卫生机构101.6万个，其中乡镇卫生院3.4万个，社区卫生服务中心（站）3.7万个，门诊部（所）36.2万个，村卫生室58.3万个；专业公共卫生机构1.2万个，其中疾病预防控制中心3426个，卫生监督所（中心）2791个。卫生技术人员1247万人，其中执业医师和执

[73] 特种影片是指采用与常规影院放映在技术、设备、节目方面不同的电影展示方式，如巨幕电影、立体特效（4D）电影、动感电影、球幕电影等。

[74] 人均图书拥有量是指在一年内全国平均每人能拥有的当年出版图书册数。

业助理医师478万人，注册护士563万人。医疗卫生机构床位1020万张，其中医院800万张，乡镇卫生院151万张。全年总诊疗人次[75]95.6亿人次，出院人次[76]3.0亿人次。

图23 2019-2023年年末卫生技术人员人数

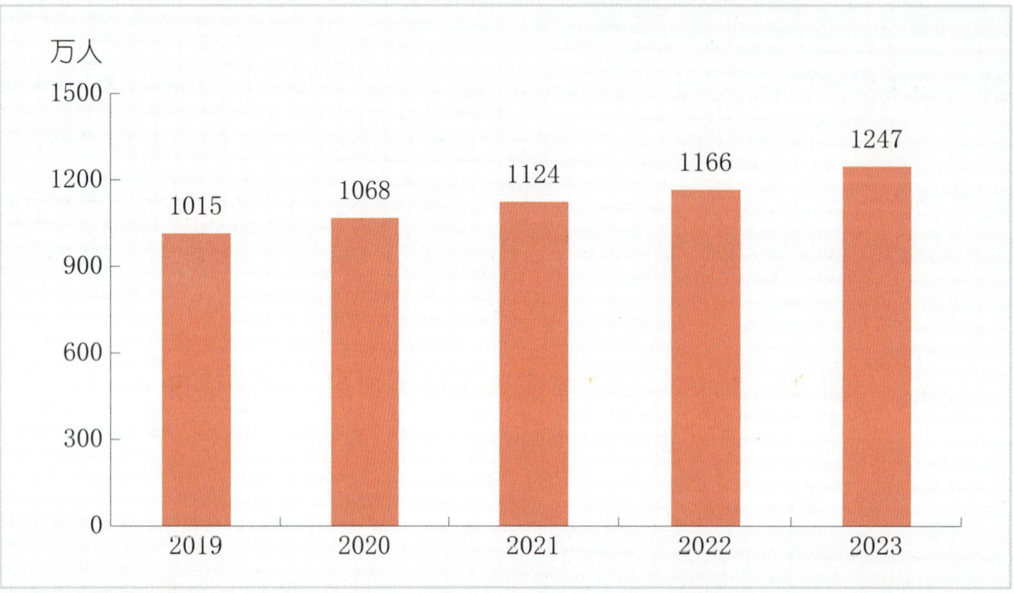

年末全国共有体育场地[77]459.3万个，体育场地面积[78]40.7亿平方米，人均体育场地面积2.89平方米。全年我国运动员在32个项目中获得165个世界冠军，共创20项世界纪录。在杭州第19届亚运会上，我国运动员共获得201枚金牌，奖牌总数383枚，第11次蝉联亚运会金牌榜首位。我国残疾人运动员在45项国际赛事中获得231个世界冠军。在杭州第4届亚残运会上，我国运动员共获得214枚金牌，奖牌总数521枚，第4次蝉联亚残运会金牌榜和奖牌榜首位。

十二、资源、环境和应急管理

全年全国国有建设用地供应总量[79]74.9万公顷，比上年下降2.1%。其中，工矿仓储用地17.5万公顷，下降11.9%；房地产用地[80]8.4万公顷，下降23.3%；基础设施用地49.0万公顷，增长7.2%。

全年水资源总量24780亿立方米。总用水量5907亿立方米，比上年下降1.5%。其中，生活用水增长0.5%，工业用水增长0.2%，农业用水下降2.9%，人工生态环境补水增长3.9%。万元国内生产

[75] 总诊疗人次是指所有诊疗工作的总人次数，包括门诊、急诊、出诊、预约诊疗、单项健康检查、健康咨询指导（不含健康讲座、核酸检测）人次数。

[76] 出院人次是指报告期内所有住院后出院的人次数，包括医嘱离院、医嘱转其他医疗机构、非医嘱离院、死亡及其他人次数，不含家庭病床撤床人次数。

[77] 体育场地调查对象不包括军队、铁路系统所属体育场地。

[78] 体育场地面积是指体育训练、比赛、健身场地的有效面积。

[79] 国有建设用地供应总量是指报告期内市、县人民政府根据年度土地供应计划依法以出让、划拨、租赁等方式与用地单位或个人签订出让合同或签发划拨决定书、完成交易的国有建设用地总量。

[80] 房地产用地是指商服用地和住宅用地的总和。

总值用水量[81]50立方米，下降6.4%。万元工业增加值用水量26立方米，下降3.9%。人均用水量419立方米，下降1.4%。

全年完成造林面积400万公顷，其中人工造林面积133万公顷，占全部造林面积的33.4%。种草改良面积[82]438万公顷。截至年末，共有国家公园5个。全年新增水土流失治理面积6.3万平方公里。

初步核算，全年能源消费总量57.2亿吨标准煤，比上年增长5.7%。煤炭消费量增长5.6%，原油消费量增长9.1%，天然气消费量增长7.2%，电力消费量增长6.7%。煤炭消费量占能源消费总量比重为55.3%，比上年下降0.7个百分点；天然气、水电、核电、风电、太阳能发电等清洁能源消费量占能源消费总量比重为26.4%，上升0.4个百分点。重点耗能工业企业单位电石综合能耗下降0.8%，单位合成氨综合能耗上升0.9%，吨钢综合能耗上升1.6%，单位电解铝综合能耗下降0.1%，每千瓦时火力发电标准煤耗下降0.2%。初步测算，扣除原料用能和非化石能源消费量后，全国万元国内生产总值能耗[83]比上年下降0.5%。全国碳排放权交易市场碳排放配额[84]成交量2.12亿吨，成交额144.4亿元。

图 24　2019-2023 年清洁能源消费量占能源消费总量的比重

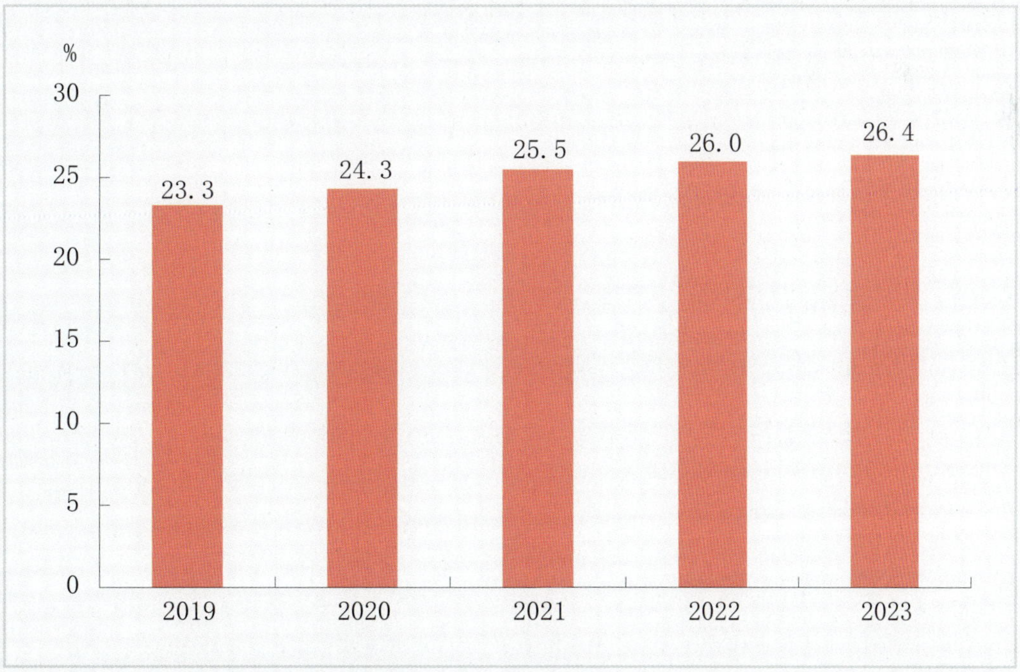

[81] 万元国内生产总值用水量、万元工业增加值用水量按2020年价格计算。
[82] 种草改良面积是指通过人工种草、飞播种草、草原改良、围栏封育等措施进行草原生态修复的面积之和。
[83] 万元国内生产总值能耗按2020年价格计算。
[84] 全国碳排放权交易市场碳排放配额是指在全国碳排放权交易市场分配给重点排放单位规定时期内的二氧化碳等温室气体的排放额度。

全年近岸海域海水水质[85]达到国家一、二类海水水质标准的面积占85.0%，三类海水占4.5%，四类、劣四类海水占10.5%。

在监测的339个地级及以上城市中，细颗粒物（$PM_{2.5}$）年平均浓度30微克/立方米，比上年上升3.4%。

在开展城市区域声环境昼间监测的326个城市中，全年声环境质量好的城市占5.8%，较好的占69.3%，一般的占23.9%，较差的占0.9%，无差的城市。

全年平均气温为10.71℃，比上年上升0.21℃。共有6个台风登陆。

全年农作物受灾面积1054万公顷，其中绝收98万公顷。因洪涝和地质灾害造成直接经济损失2451亿元，因干旱灾害造成直接经济损失206亿元，因低温冷冻和雪灾造成直接经济损失49亿元，因海洋灾害造成直接经济损失25亿元。共发生5.0级以上地震11次，造成直接经济损失153亿元。共发生森林火灾328起，受害森林面积约0.4万公顷。

全年各类生产安全事故共死亡21242人，比上年下降[86]4.7%。工矿商贸企业就业人员10万人生产安全事故死亡人数1.244人，比上年上升4.2%；煤矿百万吨死亡人数0.094人，上升23.7%。道路交通事故万车死亡人数1.38人，下降5.5%。

[85] 近岸海域海水水质采用面积法进行评价。
[86] 2022年生产安全事故统计数据进行了核实调整，2023年与上年对比按照调整后数据计算。

资料来源：

本公报中城镇新增就业、养老保险、失业保险、工伤保险、中等职业教育中的技工学校数据来自人力资源和社会保障部；外汇储备、汇率数据来自国家外汇管理局；经营主体、质量检验、国家标准制定修订、制造业产品质量合格率数据来自国家市场监督管理总局；环境监测、碳排放权交易数据来自生态环境部；水产品产量、新建和改造提升高标准农田面积、新增高效节水灌溉面积数据来自农业农村部；木材产量、造林面积、种草改良面积、国家公园数据来自国家林业和草原局；水资源总量、用水量、新增水土流失治理面积数据来自水利部；发电装机容量、新增220千伏及以上交流变电设备容量、电力消费量数据来自中国电力企业联合会；港口货物吞吐量、港口集装箱吞吐量、公路运输、水路运输、新改建高速公路里程、港口万吨级及以上码头泊位新增通过能力数据来自交通运输部；铁路运输、新建铁路投产里程、增新建铁路复线投产里程、电气化铁路投产里程数据来自中国国家铁路集团有限公司；民航运输、新增民用运输机场数据来自中国民用航空局；管道运输数据来自中国石油天然气集团有限公司、中国石油化工集团有限公司、中国海洋石油集团有限公司、国家石油天然气管网集团有限公司；民用汽车保有量、道路交通事故数据来自公安部；邮政业务数据来自国家邮政局；通信业、软件业务收入、新增光缆线路长度数据来自工业和信息化部；互联网上网人数、互联网普及率数据来自中国互联网络信息中心；二手房交易网签面积、棚户区改造、保障性租赁住房、城镇老旧小区改造数据来自住房和城乡建设部；货物进出口数据来自海关总署；服务进出口、外商直接投资、对外直接投资、对外承包工程、对外劳务合作数据来自商务部；财政数据来自财政部；新增减税降费及退税缓费数据来自国家税务总局；货币金融、公司信用类债券数据来自中国人民银行；境内交易场所筹资数据来自中国证券监督管理委员会；保险业数据来自国家金融监督管理总局；医疗保险、生育保险数据来自国家医疗保障局；城乡低保、农村特困人员救助供养、临时救助、民政服务数据来自民政部；优抚对象数据来自退役军人事务部；国家自然科学基金资助项目数据来自国家自然科学基金委员会；国家科技成果转化引导基金、国家级科技企业孵化器、国家备案众创空间、技术合同数据来自科学技术部；国家工程研究中心、国家企业技术中心数据来自国家发展和改革委员会；专利、商标数据来自国家知识产权局；公民具备科学素质比例数据来自中国科学技术协会；宇航发射数据来自国家国防科技工业局；教育数据来自教育部；艺术表演团体、公共图书馆、文化馆、旅游数据来自文化和旅游部；电视、广播数据来自国家广播电视总局；电影数据来自国家电影局；报纸、期刊、图书数据来自国家新闻出版署；档案数据来自国家档案局；居民出境数据来自国家移民管理局；医疗卫生数据来自国家卫生健康委员会；卫生监督数据来自国家疾病预防控制局；体育数据来自国家体育总局；残疾人运动员数据来自中国残疾人联合会；国有建设用地供应、海洋灾害造成直接经济损失数据来自自然资源部；平均气温、台风登陆数据来自中国气象局；农作物受灾面积、洪涝和地质灾害造成直接经济损失、干旱灾害造成直接经济损失、低温冷冻和雪灾造成直接经济损失、地震次数、地震灾害造成直接经济损失、森林火灾、受害森林面积、生产安全事故数据来自应急管理部；其他数据均来自国家统计局。

STATISTICAL COMMUNIQUÉ OF THE PEOPLE'S REPUBLIC OF CHINA ON THE 2023 NATIONAL ECONOMIC AND SOCIAL DEVELOPMENT[1]

National Bureau of Statistics of China
February 29, 2024

The year 2023 is the first year to fully implement the guiding principles of the 20th National Congress of the Communist Party of China (CPC) and a year for economic recovery and development following three years of COVID-19 prevention and control. Faced with complex and grave international environment as well as arduous tasks to advance reform, promote development and maintain stability at home, under the strong leadership of the CPC Central Committee with Comrade Xi Jinping at its core, all regions and departments took Xi Jinping Thought on Socialism with Chinese Characteristics for a New Era as the guideline, fully implemented the guiding principles of the 20th CPC National Congress and the Second Plenary Session of the 20th CPC Central Committee, followed the decisions and arrangements made by the CPC Central Committee and the State Council, adhered to the general working guideline of making progress while

1. All figures in this Communiqué are preliminary statistics. Statistics in this Communiqué do not include Hong Kong SAR, Macao SAR and Taiwan Province. Due to the rounding-off reasons, the subentries may not add up to the aggregate totals.

maintaining stability, fully and faithfully applied the new development philosophy on all fronts, accelerated efforts to foster a new pattern of development, strove to promote high-quality development, comprehensively deepened reform and opening up, strengthened macro control, and redoubled efforts to expand domestic demand, optimize structure, boost confidence and prevent and defuse risks. As a result, the national economy witnessed the momentum of recovery. The high-quality development was pursued with solid steps, important advancement was achieved in the building of a modern industrial system, new breakthroughs were made in scientific and technological innovation, reform and opening-up was deepened, the foundation for security and development was consolidated, people's wellbeing was strongly and effectively guaranteed, social harmony and stability was achieved, and solid strides were taken in building a modern socialist country in all respects.

I. General Outlook

According to preliminary estimation, the gross domestic product (GDP)[2] in 2023 was 126,058.2 billion yuan, up by 5.2 percent over the previous year. Of this total, the value added of the primary industry was 8,975.5 billion yuan, up by 4.1 percent over the previous year, that of the secondary industry was 48,258.9 billion yuan, up by 4.7 percent, and that of the tertiary industry was 68,823.8 billion yuan, up by 5.8 percent. The value added of the primary industry accounted for 7.1 percent of the GDP; that of the secondary industry accounted for 38.3 percent; and that of the tertiary industry accounted for 54.6 percent. The contribution of the final consumption expenditure to GDP growth rate was up by 4.3 percentage points, that of the gross capital formation to GDP growth rate up by 1.5 percentage points and that of the net exports of goods and services to GDP growth rate down by 0.6 percentage points. By quarter, the GDP for the first quarter went up by 4.5 percent year on year, up by 6.3 percent for the second quarter, 4.9 percent for the third quarter and 5.2 percent for the fourth quarter. The per capita GDP in 2023 was 89,358 yuan, up by 5.4 percent over the previous year. The gross national income[3] in 2023 was 125,129.7 billion yuan, up by 5.6 percent over the previous year. The overall labor productivity[4] was 161,615 yuan per person, up by 5.7 percent over the previous year.

---

2. Gross domestic product (GDP), value added of the three and related industries, regional GDP, per capita GDP and gross national income (GNI) as quoted in this Communiqué are calculated at current prices whereas their growth rates are at constant prices.

3. Gross national income, also known as gross national product, refers to the total primary distribution of the income created by all the resident units of a country (or a region) during a certain period of time. It equals to gross domestic product plus the net primary distribution of income from abroad.

4. The overall labor productivity refers to the ratio between the GDP (at 2020 constant prices) and the total number of persons employed.

Figure 1: Gross Domestic Product and Growth Rates 2019-2023

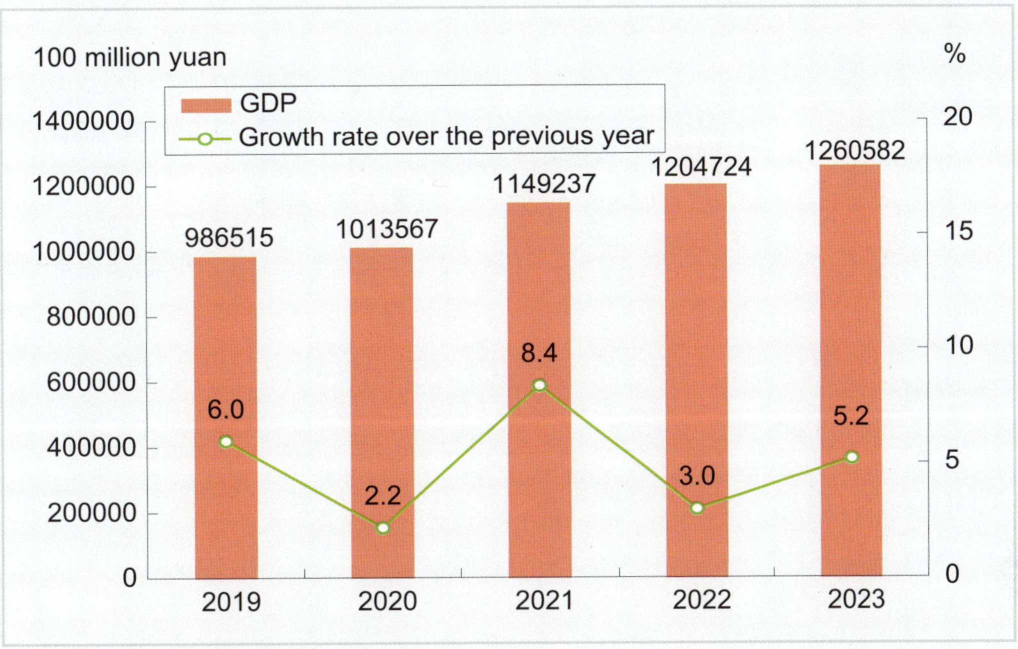

Figure 2: Shares of the Three Industries' Value Added in GDP 2019-2023

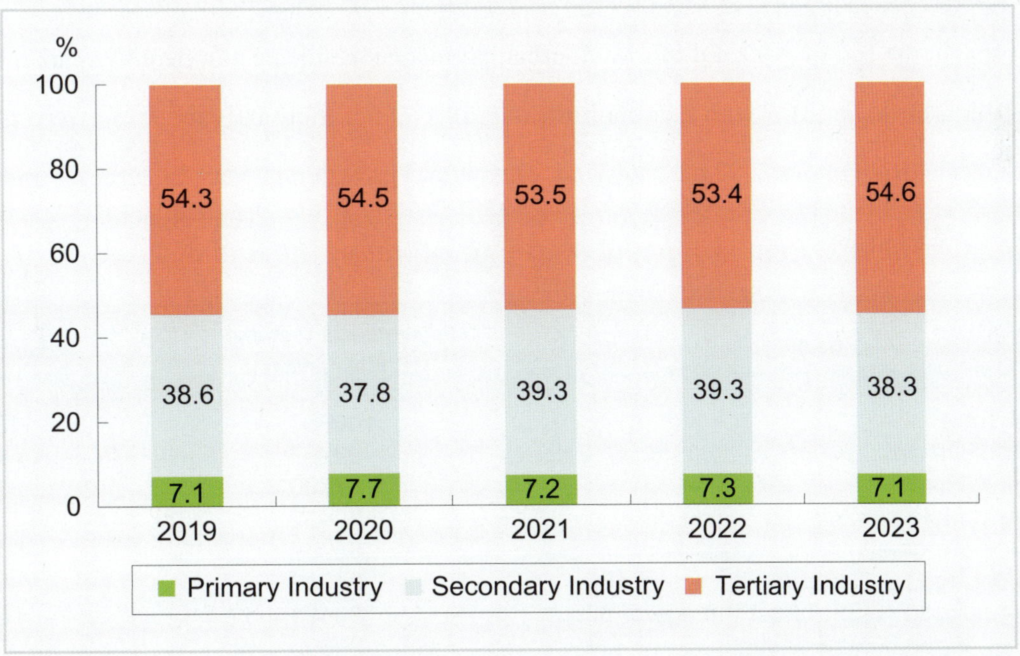

Figure 3: The Overall Labor Productivity 2019-2023

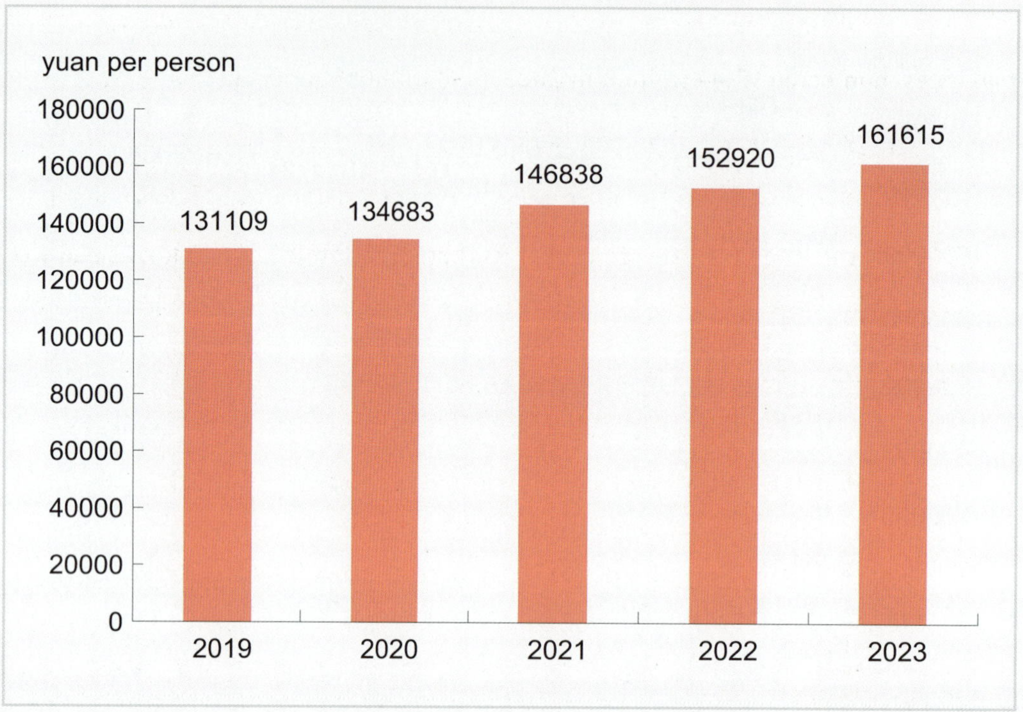

By the end of 2023, the total number of national population[5] reached 1,409.67 million, a decrease of 2.08 million over that at the end of 2022. Of this total, urban permanent residents numbered 932.67 million. There were 9.02 million births in 2023 with a crude birth rate of 6.39 per thousand; and there were 11.10 million deaths with a crude death rate of 7.87 per thousand. The natural growth rate was -1.48 per thousand.

Table 1: Population and Its Composition by the End of 2023

Item	Population at Year-end (10,000 persons)	Proportion (%)
National Total	**140967**	**100.0**
Of which: Urban	93267	66.2
Rural	47700	33.8
Of which: Male	72032	51.1
Female	68935	48.9
Of which: Aged 0-15 (under the age of 16)[6]	24789	17.6
Aged 16-59 (under the age of 60)	86481	61.3
Aged 60 and above	29697	21.1
Of which: Aged 65 and above	21676	15.4

5. The national population refers to the population of the 31 provinces, autonomous regions and municipalities directly under the central government and servicemen of the Chinese mainland, excluding residents of Hong Kong, Macao and Taiwan and foreigners living in the 31 provinces, autonomous regions and municipalities directly under the central government.

6. By the end of 2023, the population aged 0 to 14 (under the age of 15) was 230.63 million and that aged 15 to 59 (under the age of 60) was 882.07 million.

At the end of 2023, the number of employed people in China was 740.41 million, and that in urban areas was 470.32 million, accounting for 63.5 percent of the total employed people. The newly increased employed people in urban areas[7] numbered 12.44 million in 2023, 0.38 million more than that of the previous year. The urban surveyed unemployment rate in 2023 averaged 5.2 percent. The urban surveyed unemployment rate at the year end was 5.1 percent. The total number of migrant workers[8] was 297.53 million, up by 0.6 percent over that of 2022. Specifically, the number of migrant workers who left their hometowns and worked in other places was 176.58 million, up by 2.7 percent, and those who worked in their own localities reached 120.95 million, down by 2.2 percent.

Figure 4: Newly Increased Employed People in Urban Areas 2019-2023

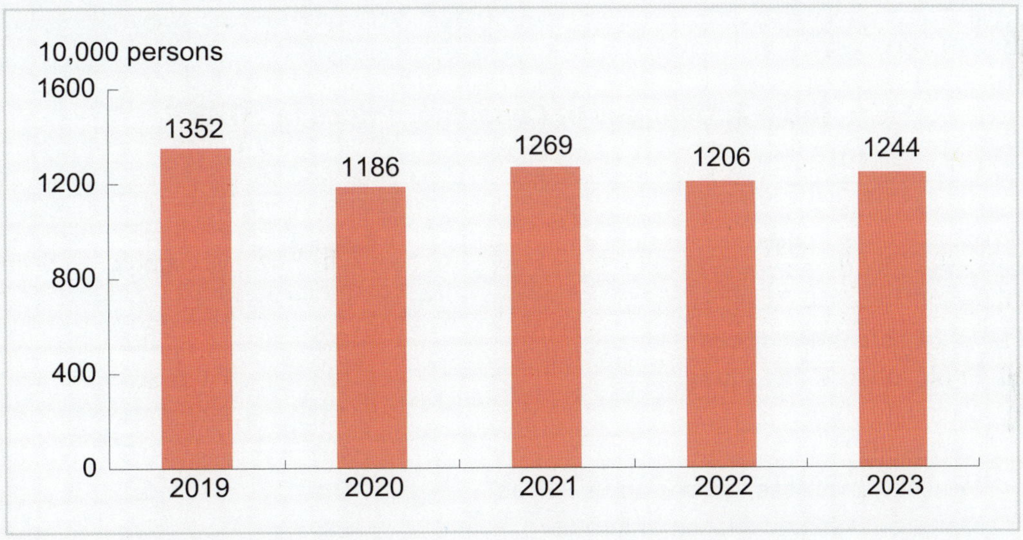

The consumer prices in 2023 went up by 0.2 percent over the previous year. The producer prices for industrial products went down by 3.0 percent and the purchasing prices for industrial producers down by 3.6 percent. The producer prices for farm products[9] dropped by 2.3 percent. In December, out of the 70 large and medium-sized cities, 20 cities experienced a year-on-year rise in sales prices of new commercial residential buildings, 2 cities maintained the same and 48 cities experienced a decline; one city experienced a year-on-year rise in sales prices of second-hand housing, and 69 cities experienced a decline.

---

7. The number of newly increased employed people in urban areas equals the number of cumulative new employment minus the number of natural attrition in urban areas during the reporting period.

8. The number of migrant workers includes those who are employed outside their villages and towns for more than six months in the year and those who are engaged in non-agricultural work in their villages and towns for more than six months in the year.

9. The producer prices for farm products refer to the prices of farm products sold firsthand by producers.

Figure 5: Monthly Changes of Consumer Prices in 2023

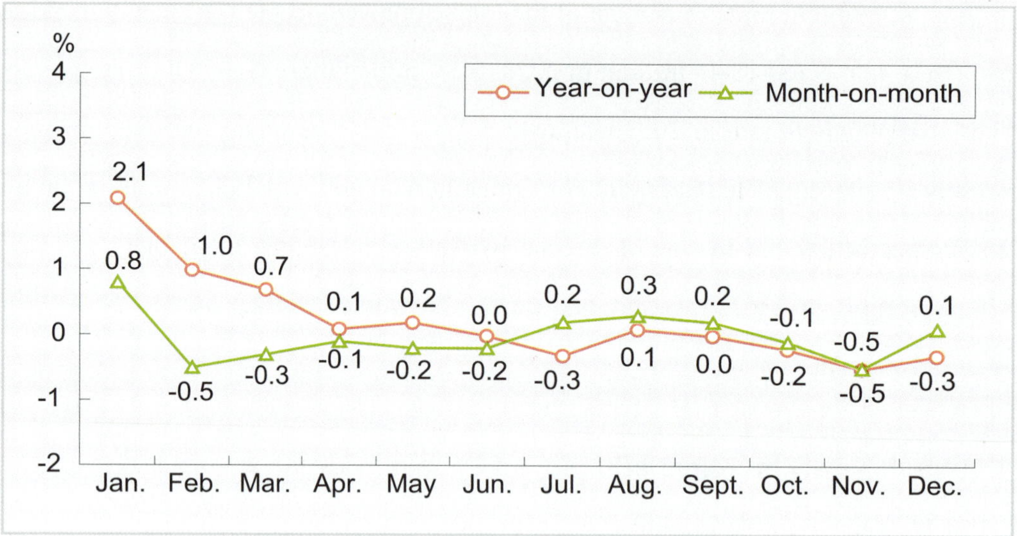

Table 2: Changes of Consumer Prices in 2023

Unit: %

Item	National	Urban	Rural
General level of consumer prices	**0.2**	**0.3**	**0.1**
Of which: Food, tobacco and liquor	0.3	0.4	0.1
Clothing	1.0	1.1	0.6
Residence[10]	0.0	0.0	0.0
Household facilities, articles and services	0.1	0.1	-0.1
Transportation and telecommunication	-2.3	-2.3	-2.4
Education, culture and recreation	2.0	2.1	1.5
Health care and medical services	1.1	1.1	1.3
Miscellaneous goods and services	3.2	3.4	2.5

At the end of 2023, China's foreign exchange reserves reached 3,238.0 billion US dollars, an increase of 110.3 billion US dollars compared with that at the end of 2022. The average exchange rate of the year was 7.0467 RMB to 1 USD dollar, depreciated by 4.5 percent over that of 2022.

10. The prices for residence include prices for rent, maintenance and management, water, electricity and fuel, and services for owner-occupied housing etc.

Figure 6: Year-end China's Foreign Exchange Reserves 2019-2023

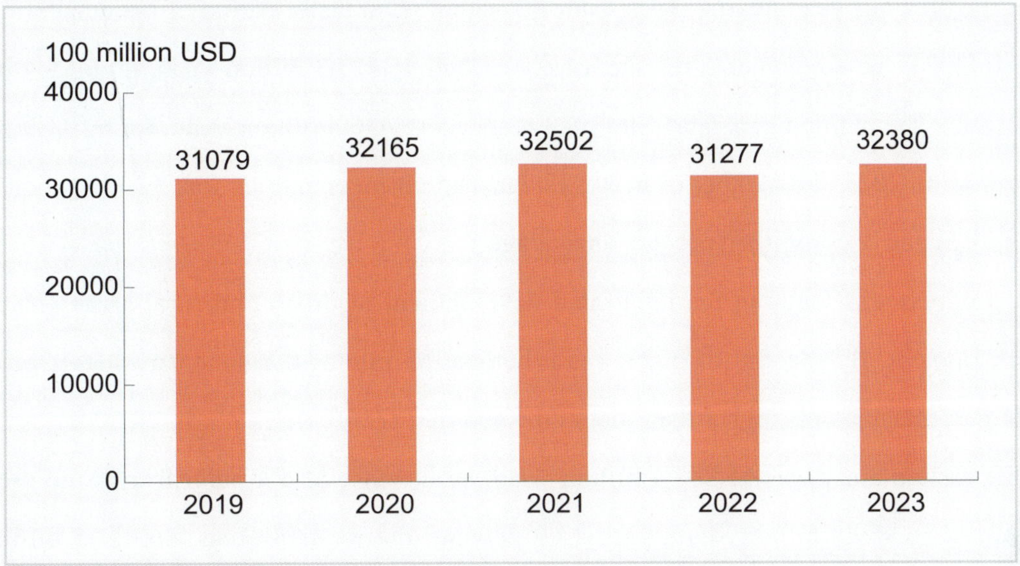

New growth drivers witnessed robust development. Among the industries above the designated size[11], the value added of the manufacture of equipment[12] was up by 6.8 percent over the previous year, accounting for 33.6 percent of that of all industrial enterprises above the designated size. The value added of the high technology manufacturing industry[13] increased by 2.7 percent, accounting for 15.7 percent of that of all industrial enterprises above the designated size. In 2023, the output of new energy vehicles reached 9.443 million, up by 30.3 percent over the previous year; that of solar cells (photovoltaic cells) was 0.54 billion kilowatts, up by 54.0 percent; that of service robots reached 7.833 million, up by 23.3 percent; and that of 3D printing devices totaled 2.789 million, up by 36.2 percent. Among the service enterprises above the designated size[14], the business revenue of the strategic emerging service industries[15] went up by 7.7 percent

11. The growth rates and rate changes of relevant indicators of the industries above the designated size in 2023 were calculated on a comparable basis due to adjustments of survey coverage in the statistical survey programs, statistical law enforcement and removal of duplicated data.

12. Manufacture of equipment includes manufacture of metal products, general purpose equipment, special purpose equipment, automobiles, railway, ship, aerospace and other transport equipment, electrical machinery and apparatus, computers, communication and other electric equipment and measuring instrument and machinery.

13. High technology manufacturing industry includes manufacture of medicine, manufacture of aerospace vehicle and equipment, manufacture of electronic and communication equipment, manufacture of computers and office equipment, manufacture of médical equipment, manufacture of measuring instrument and equipment and manufacture of optical and photographic equipment.

14. Service enterprises above the designated size refer to legal entities of transport, storage and post, information transmission, software and information technology services, water conservancy, environment and public facilities management, and health with annual business revenue of 20 million yuan and above; legal entities of real estate (excluding real estate development and operation), leasing and business services, scientific research and technology services and education with annual business revenue of 10 million yuan and above; and legal entities of services to households, repair and other services and culture, sports and entertainment, and social services with annual business revenue of 5 million and above. The growth rates of financial indicators of service enterprises above the designated size in 2023 were calculated on a comparable basis.

15. Strategic emerging service industries refer to the related service sectors of information technology of new generation, manufacture of high-end equipment, new materials, biotech, new energy vehicles, new energy, energy-saving and environmental protection and digital creative industries, and service industries related to new technology, innovation and entrepreneurship.

compared with the previous year. In 2023, the investment in high technology industries[16] increased by 10.3 percent over the previous year and the investment in technology transformation of manufacturing[17] grew by 3.8 percent. In 2023, the e-commerce transactions[18] reached 46,827.3 billion yuan, up by 9.4 percent over the previous year. The online retail sales[19] in 2023 reached 15,426.4 billion yuan, up by 11.0 percent over the previous year. In 2023, the number of newly established business entities was 32.73 million, with 0.027 million enterprises newly established per day on average.

Steady progress was made in the integrated development of urban and rural areas and coordinated regional development. By the end of 2023, the urbanization rate of permanent residents reached 66.16 percent, 0.94 percentage points higher than that at the end of 2022. By region[20], in 2023, the gross domestic product in the eastern areas was 65,208.4 billion yuan, an increase of 5.4 percent over the previous year; the central areas, 26,989.8 billion yuan, up by 4.9 percent; the western areas, 26,932.5 billion yuan, up by 5.5 percent; and the northeastern areas, 5,962.4 billion yuan, up by 4.8 percent. In 2023, the gross domestic product in Beijing-Tianjin-Hebei Region reached 10,444.2 billion yuan, up by 5.1 percent over the previous year; that in the Yangtze River Economic Belt, 58,427.4 billion yuan, up by 5.5 percent; and that in the Yangtze River Delta, 30,504.5 billion yuan, up by 5.7 percent. Major regional strategies such as the construction of Guangdong-Hong Kong-Macao Greater Bay Areas, and the ecological protection and high-quality development of the Yellow River Basin were further advanced.

---

16. Investment in high technology industries refers to investment in six high technology manufacturing industries, including the manufacture of medicine and manufacture of aerospace vehicle and equipment, and nine high technology service industries, including information service and e-commerce service.

17. The investment in technology transformation of manufacturing refers to the investment by manufacturing enterprises in transformation of existing facilities, techniques and production services by adopting new technologies, techniques, devices and materials.

18. E-commerce transactions refer to the transactions of goods and services realized through e-commerce trading platforms (including self-built and third-party platforms), including transactions with entities and individuals. The growth rate of 2023 was calculated on a comparable basis.

19. Online retail sales refer to the retail sales of goods and services realized through internet trading platforms (online platforms mainly in trading physical commodities, including self-built websites and third-party platforms). The growth rate of 2023 was calculated on a comparable basis.

20. The eastern areas include 10 provinces and municipalities: Beijing, Tianjin, Hebei, Shanghai, Jiangsu, Zhejiang, Fujian, Shandong, Guangdong and Hainan; the central areas cover 6 provinces: Shanxi, Anhui, Jiangxi, Henan, Hubei and Hunan; the western areas include 12 provinces, autonomous regions and municipalities: Inner Mongolia, Guangxi, Chongqing, Sichuan, Guizhou, Yunnan, Tibet, Shaanxi, Gansu, Qinghai, Ningxia and Xinjiang; the northeastern areas include 3 provinces: Liaoning, Jilin and Heilongjiang.

Figure 7: Year-end Urbanization Rates of Permanent Residents 2019-2023

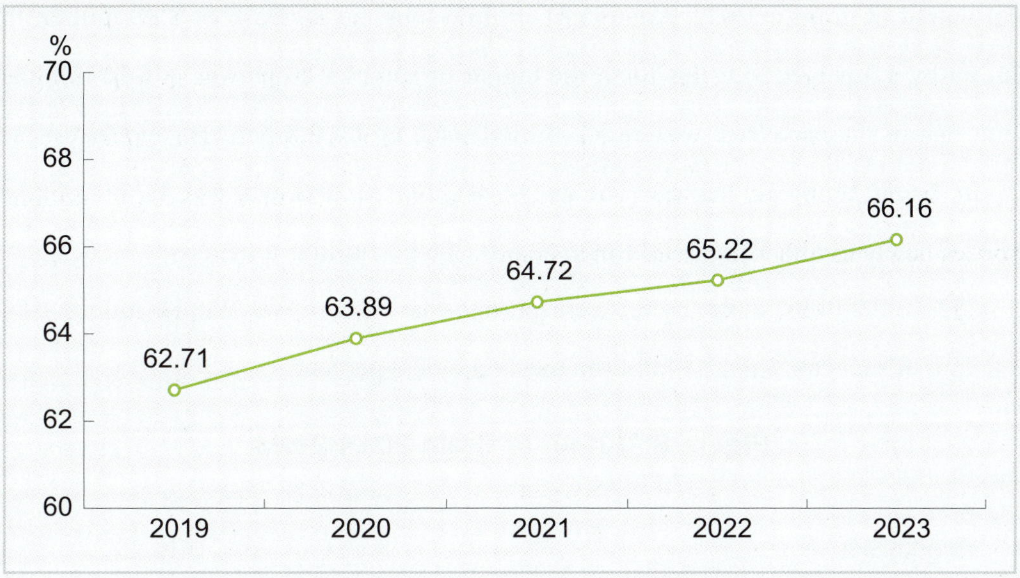

Green and low-carbon transformation was further promoted. The national carbon dioxide emissions per 10,000 yuan worth of GDP[21] in 2023 remained the same as that of the previous year. In 2023, the electricity generated by clean energy such as hydropower, nuclear power, wind power and solar power was 3,190.6 billion kilowatts-hours, up by 7.8 percent over the previous year. Of the monitored 339 cities at prefecture level and above, 59.9 percent reached the air quality standard and 40.1 percent failed. Of the 3,641 sections under the national monitoring program for surface water, 89.4 percent were of fairly clean water quality (Grade I to III), 8.4 percent were Grade IV, 1.5 percent were Grade V and 0.7 percent were worse than Grade V national standard.

II. Agriculture

In 2023, the sown area of grain was 118.97 million hectares, an increase of 0.64 million hectares compared with that in 2022. Of this total, the sown area of rice was 28.95 million hectares, a decrease of 0.50 million hectares; the sown area of wheat was 23.63 million hectares, an increase of 0.11 million hectares; the sown area of corn was 44.22 million hectares, an increase of 1.15 million hectares; the sown area of soybean was 10.47 million hectares, an increase of 0.23 million hectares. The sown area of cotton was 2.79 million hectares, a decrease of 0.21 million hectares. The sown area of oil-bearing crops was 13.92 million hectares, an increase of 0.78 million hectares; the sown area of sugar crops was 1.42 million hectares, a decrease of 0.03

21. The carbon dioxide emissions per 10,000 yuan worth of GDP was calculated at 2020 constant prices.

million hectares.

The total output of grain in 2023 was 695.41 million tons, an increase of 8.88 million tons over the previous year, up by 1.3 percent. Of this total, the output of summer crops was 146.15 million tons, down by 0.8 percent, that of the early rice was 28.34 million tons, up by 0.8 percent, and that of autumn grain was 520.92 million tons, up by 1.9 percent. The output of cereal in 2023 was 641.43 million tons, up by 1.3 percent over 2022, among which the output of rice was 206.60 million tons, down by 0.9 percent; that of wheat was 136.59 million tons, down by 0.8 percent; and that of corn was 288.84 million tons, up by 4.2 percent. The output of soybean was 20.84 million tons, up by 2.8 percent.

Figure 8: Output of Grain 2019-2023

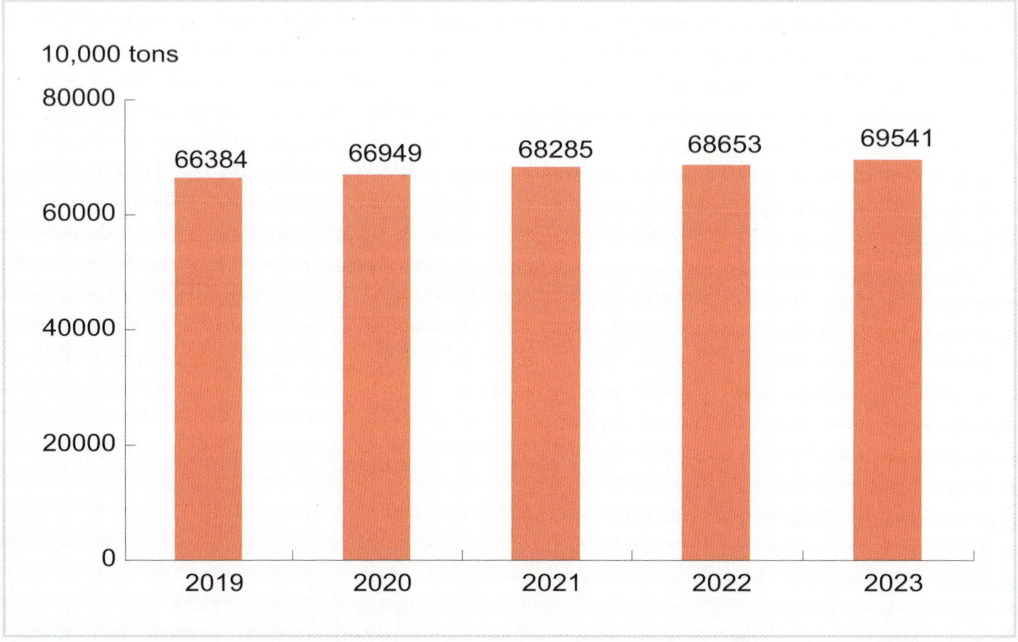

In 2023, the output of cotton was 5.62 million tons, down by 6.1 percent over the previous year, that of oil-bearing crops was 38.64 million tons, up by 5.7 percent, that of sugar crops was 115.04 million tons, up by 2.4 percent, and that of tea was 3.55 million tons, up by 6.1 percent.

The total output of pork, beef, mutton and poultry in 2023 was 96.41 million tons, up by 4.5 percent over the previous year. Of this total, the output of pork was 57.94 million tons, up by 4.6 percent; that of beef was 7.53 million tons, up by 4.8 percent; that of mutton was 5.31 million tons, up by 1.3 percent; and that of poultry was 25.63 million tons, up by 4.9 percent. The total output of eggs was 35.63 million tons, up by 3.1 percent. The output of milk was 41.97 million tons, up by 6.7 percent. At the end of the year, 434.22 million pigs were registered in the total stocks, down by 4.1 percent compared with that at the end of 2022, and

726.62 million pigs were slaughtered, up by 3.8 percent over the previous year.

The total output of aquatic products in 2023 was 71.00 million tons, up by 3.4 percent over the previous year. Of this total, the output of cultured aquatic products was 58.12 million tons, up by 4.4 percent; and that of fished aquatic products was 12.88 million tons, down by 1.0 percent.

The total production of timber in 2023 reached 119.44 million cubic meters, down by 2.0 percent over the previous year.

In 2023, the number of high-standard farmland newly developed and upgraded was 5.74 million hectares and 1.64 million hectares of farmland was newly equipped with water-saving irrigation systems.

III. Industry and Construction

In 2023, the total value added of the industrial sector was 39,910.3 billion yuan, up by 4.2 percent over the previous year. The value added of industrial enterprises above the designated size increased by 4.6 percent. Of the industrial enterprises above the designated size, in terms of ownership, the value added of the state-holding enterprises was up by 5.0 percent, that of the share-holding enterprises up by 5.3 percent, that of the enterprises funded by foreign investors and investors from Hong Kong, Macao and Taiwan up by 1.4 percent and that of private enterprises up by 3.1 percent. In terms of sectors, the value added of the mining industry was up by 2.3 percent, that of manufacturing up by 5.0 percent and that of production and supply of electricity, heat power, gas and water up by 4.3 percent.

Figure 9: Value Added and Growth Rates of Industrial Enterprises 2019-2023

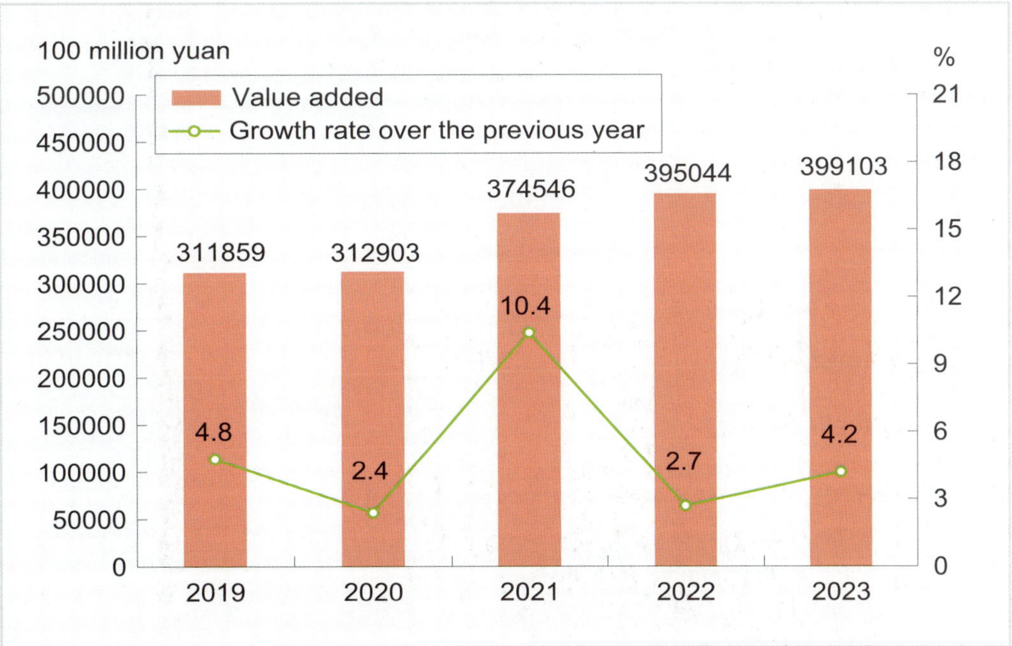

In 2023, of the industrial enterprises above the designated size, the value added for processing of food from agricultural and sideline products was up by 0.2 percent over the previous year; for textile industry down by 0.6 percent; for manufacture of raw chemical materials and chemical products up by 9.6 percent; for manufacture of non-metallic mineral products down by 0.5 percent; for smelting and pressing of ferrous metals up by 7.1 percent; for manufacture of general purpose machinery up by 2.0 percent; for manufacture of special purpose machinery up by 3.6 percent; for manufacture of automobiles up by 13.0 percent; for manufacture of electrical machinery and apparatus up by 12.9 percent; for manufacture of computers, communication equipment and other electronic equipment up by 3.4 percent; for production and supply of electricity and heat power up by 4.3 percent.

Table 3: Output of Major Industrial Products and Growth Rates of the Industrial Enterprises above the Designated Size in 2023[22]

Product	Unit	Output	Increase over 2022 (%)
Yarn	10000 tons	2234.2	-2.2
Cloth	100 million meters	294.9	-4.8
Chemical fiber	10000 tons	7127.0	10.3
Refined sugar (final product)	10000 tons	1270.6	-13.2
Cigarettes	100 million	24427.5	0.4
Color TV sets	10000	19339.6	-1.3
Household refrigerators	10000	9632.3	14.5
Air conditioners	10000	24487.0	13.5
Crude steel	10000 tons	101908.1	0.0
Rolled steel[23]	10000 tons	136268.2	5.2
Ten kinds of nonferrous metals	10000 tons	7469.8	7.1
Of which: Refined copper (copper)	10000 tons	1298.8	13.5
Aluminum electrolyze	10000 tons	4159.4	3.7
Cement	100 million tons	20.2	-0.7
Sulfuric acid (100%)	10000 tons	9580.0	3.4
Caustic soda (100%)	10000 tons	4101.4	3.5
Ethylene	10000 tons	3189.9	6.0
Chemical fertilizer (100 percent equivalent)	10000 tons	5713.6	5.0
Power generation equipment	10000 kilowatts	23442.7	28.5
Motor vehicles	10000	3011.3	9.3
Of which: New energy vehicles	10000	944.3	30.3
Large and medium tractors	10000	38.0	-7.2
Integrated circuits	100 million pieces	3514.4	6.9
Program-controlled switchboards	10000 lines	507.0	-42.6
Mobile telephones	10000	156642.2	6.9
Micro computer equipment	10000	33056.9	-17.4
Industrial robots	10000 sets	43.0	-2.2
Ultra-clear glass for solar industry	10000 square meters	159264.8	58.6
Charging piles	10000	287.8	36.9

22. See Note 11.
23. The data included the steel reprocessed among enterprises.

In 2023, the profits made by industrial enterprises above the designated size were 7,685.8 billion yuan, down by 2.3 percent over the previous year. By ownership, the profits of state-holding enterprises were 2,262.3 billion yuan, down by 3.4 percent over the previous year; those of share-holding enterprises were 5,677.3 billion yuan, down by 1.2 percent; those of enterprises funded by foreign investors and investors from Hong Kong, Macao and Taiwan were 1,797.5 billion yuan, down by 6.7 percent; and those of private enterprises were 2,343.8 billion yuan, up by 2.0 percent. In terms of different sectors, the profits of mining were 1,239.2 billion yuan, down by 19.7 percent over the previous year; those of manufacturing were 5,764.4 billion yuan, down by 2.0 percent; and those of the production and supply of electricity, heat power, gas and water were 682.2 billion yuan, up by 54.7 percent. The cost for per-hundred-yuan business revenue of the industrial enterprises above the designated size was 84.76 yuan, 0.04 yuan more than that of 2022; the profit rate of the business revenue was 5.76 percent, 0.20 percentage points down. By the end of 2023, the asset-liability ratio of industrial enterprises above the designated size was 57.1 percent, 0.1 percentage points lower than that at the end of 2022. The capacity utilization rate[24] of industrial enterprises above the designated size was 75.1 percent in 2023.

According to preliminary estimates, the total primary energy output in 2023 was 4.83 billion tons of standard coal equivalent, up by 4.2 percent over that of the previous year.

Table 4: Output of Major Energy Products and Growth Rates in 2023

Product	Unit	Output	Increase over 2022(%)
Coal	100 million tons	47.1	3.4
Crude petroleum oil	10000 tons	20902.6	2.1
Natural gas	100 million cubic meters	2324.3	5.6
Electricity	100 million kilowatt-hours	94564.4	6.9
Of which: Thermal power[25]	100 million kilowatt-hours	62657.4	6.4
Hydropower	100 million kilowatt-hours	12858.5	-4.9
Nuclear-power	100 million kilowatt-hours	4347.2	4.1
Wind power	100 million kilowatt-hours	8858.7	16.2
Solar power	100 million kilowatt-hours	5841.5	36.7

24. Capacity utilization rate refers to the ratio of the actual production to the production capacity (in terms of value). Actual production refers to the total industrial output value during the enterprise's reporting period. Production capacity refers to the production which can be realized and sustained for a long term under the condition of the supply of labor force, materials, fuel and transportation guaranteed and the production equipment in proper operation during the reporting period.

25. Thermal power refers to electricity generated by coal, oil, gas, residual heat, pressure and gas, waste incineration and biomass.

By the end of 2023, the installed power generation capacity was 2,919.65 million kilowatts, up by 13.9 percent over that at the end of 2022, among which[26] the installed thermal power generation capacity was 1,390.32 million kilowatts, up by 4.1 percent; the installed hydropower generation capacity was 421.54 million kilowatts, up by 1.8 percent; the installed nuclear power generation capacity was 56.91 million kilowatts, up by 2.4 percent; the installed grid-connected wind power generation capacity was 441.34 million kilowatts, up by 20.7 percent and the installed grid-connected solar power generation capacity was 609.49 million kilowatts, up by 55.2 percent.

In 2023, the value added of construction enterprises was 8,569.1 billion yuan, up by 7.1 percent over the previous year. The profits made by construction enterprises qualified for general contracts and specialized contracts reached 832.6 billion yuan, up by 0.2 percent over the previous year[27], of which the profits made by state-holding enterprises were 401.9 billion yuan, up by 4.3 percent.

Figure 10: Value Added and Growth Rates of Construction Industry 2019-2023

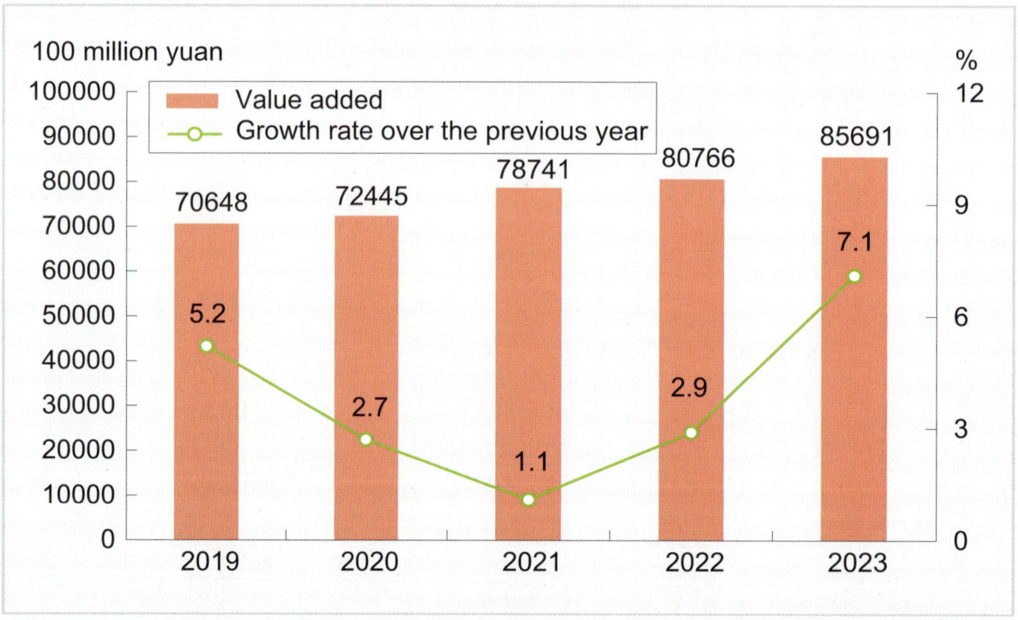

26. A few installed power generation capacity (e.g. geothermal) is not listed.

27. The growth rate of the profits made by construction enterprises was calculated on a comparable basis. Factors causing incomparability between the data of reporting period and the data released of the same period in the previous year made it impossible to calculate the growth rate directly. The main reasons were as below: ① Data of principal businesses that were not within the coverage of construction industry were removed in the data quality review. ② Problematic data were spotted and revised according to relevant rules as a result of statistical law enforcement.

IV. Service Sector

In 2023, the value added of the wholesale and retail trades was 12,307.2 billion yuan, up by 6.2 percent over the previous year; that of transport, storage and post was 5,782.0 billion yuan, up by 8.0 percent; that of hotels and catering services was 2,102.4 billion yuan, up by 14.5 percent; that of financial intermediation was 10,067.7 billion yuan, up by 6.8 percent; that of real estate was 7,372.3 billion yuan, down by 1.3 percent; that of information transmission, software and information technology services was 5,519.4 billion yuan, up by 11.9 percent; and that of leasing and business services was 4,434.7 billion yuan, up by 9.3 percent. The business revenue of service enterprises above the designated size grew by 8.3 percent over the previous year, and the total profits increased by 26.8 percent.

Figure 11: Value Added and Growth Rates of Service Sector 2019-2023

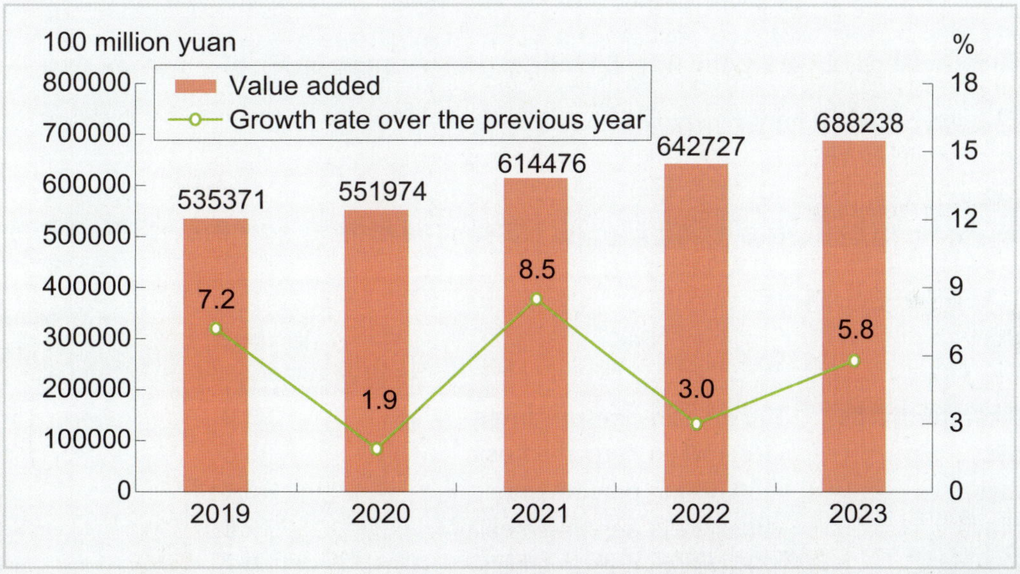

The total freight traffic[28] in 2023 reached 55.7 billion tons, up by 8.1 percent over the previous year. The freight flows were 24,771.3 billion ton-kilometers, up by 6.3 percent. The volume of freight handled by ports totaled 17.0 billion tons, up by 8.2 percent over the previous year, of which the freight for foreign trade was 5.0 billion tons, up by 9.5 percent. Container shipping of ports reached 310.34 million standard containers, up by 4.9 percent.

28. The total freight traffic and flows include the traffic and flows by railways, highways, waterways, civil aviation and pipelines and the growth rates in 2023 were calculated on a comparable basis.

Table 5: Freight Traffic by All Means of Transportation and Growth Rates in 2023

Item	Unit	Volume	Increase over 2022(%)
Total freight traffic	**100 million tons**	**556.8**	**8.1**
Railways	100 million tons	50.1	1.5
Highways	100 million tons	403.4	8.7
Waterways	100 million tons	93.7	9.5
Civil aviation	10000 tons	735.4	21.0
Pipelines	100 million tons	9.5	7.5
Freight flows	**100 million ton-kilometers**	**247712.7**	**6.3**
Railways	100 million ton-kilometers	36437.6	1.5
Highways	100 million ton-kilometers	73950.2	6.9
Waterways	100 million ton-kilometers	129951.5	7.4
Civil aviation	100 million ton-kilometers	283.6	11.6
Pipelines	100 million ton-kilometers	7089.8	3.8

In 2023, the total passenger traffic was 9.3 billion person-times, up by 66.5 percent over 2022, and the passenger flows were 2,861.0 billion person-kilometers, up by 121.4 percent.

Table 6: Passenger Traffic by All Means of Transportation and Growth Rates in 2023

Item	Unit	Volume	Increase over 2022(%)
Total passenger traffic	**100 million person-times**	**93.0**	**66.5**
Railways	100 million person-times	38.5	130.4
Highways	100 million person-times	45.7	28.9
Waterways	100 million person-times	2.6	121.6
Civil aviation	100 million person-times	6.2	146.1
Passenger flows	**100 million person-kilometers**	**28609.6**	**121.4**
Railways	100 million person-kilometers	14729.4	123.9
Highways	100 million person-kilometers	3517.6	46.1
Waterways	100 million person-kilometers	53.8	137.9
Civil aviation	100 million person-kilometers	10308.8	163.4

The total number of motor vehicles for civilian use reached 336.18 million (including 7.06 million tri-wheel motor vehicles and low-speed trucks) by the end of 2023, up by 17.14 million over that at the end of 2022, of which the privately-owned vehicles numbered 294.27 million, an increase of 15.53 million. The total number of cars for civilian use was 186.68 million, an increase of 9.28 million, of which the privately-owned cars numbered 175.41 million, an increase of 8.56 million.

In 2023, the volume of postal and delivery services[29] totaled 162.5 billion, up by 16.8 percent over the previous year. The number of mail delivery was 0.97 billion; that of parcel delivery was 0.02 billion; and that of express delivery was 132.07 billion with a revenue reaching 1,207.4 billion yuan. The turnover of telecommunication services[30] in 2023 totaled 1,832.7 billion yuan, up by 16.8 percent over the previous year. By the end of 2023, there were 11.62 million mobile phone base stations[31], among which the number of 4G base stations reached 6.29 million and that of 5G base stations was 3.38 million. There were 1,899.92 million phone subscribers in China, of whom 1,726.60 million were mobile phone subscribers. The mobile phone coverage was 122.5 sets per 100 persons. The number of fixed broadband internet users[32] reached 636.31 million, an increase of 46.66 million over that at the end of the previous year. Of this total, users of broadband with the speed of 100M and above[33] amounted to 601.36 million, an increase of 47.56 million. Users of cellular internet of things terminals[34] totaled 2.332 billion, an increase of 0.488 billion. The number of internet users was 1.092 billion, 1.091 billion of which were mobile internet surfers. The coverage of internet was 77.5 percent, and 66.5 percent in rural areas. The mobile internet traffic in 2023 was 301.5 billion gigabytes, up by 15.2 percent over the previous year. Software revenue of software and information technology services industry[35] was 12,325.8 billion yuan, up by 13.4 percent over that of the previous year.

---

29. The volume of postal and delivery services refers to the total volume of universal postal services and express delivery services provided by enterprises.

30. The turnover of telecommunication services was calculated based on the prices of the previous year.

31. The number of mobile phone base stations refers to the total number of wireless transceivers serving communities that handle the wireless communication between the base stations and mobile stations, relay between the mobile switchboards and mobile stations, and monitor the quality of wireless transmission at the end of the reporting period.

32. Fixed broadband internet users refer to those who subscribed to the telecommunication enterprises and accessed the Internet through xDSL, FTTx+LAN, FTTH/0 and other broadband access ways as well as general dedicated lines at the end of the reporting period.

33. Users of broadband with the speed of 100M and above refer to those who enjoy a downstream rate of 100Mbit/s or above at the end of the reporting period.

34. Users of cellular internet of things terminals refer to those who access the mobile internet and subscribe to the internet of things services at the end of the reporting period. Internet of things terminals refers to the internet of things devices that connect the sensing network layer and the transmission network layer to implement remote data collection and data transmission to the network layer.

35. Software and information technology services industry includes software development, integrated circuit design, information system integration and internet of things technology services, operation maintenance services, information processing and storage support services, IT consulting services, digital content services and other IT services industry. The growth rate of software revenue of software and information technology services industry in 2023 was calculated on a comparable basis.

Figure 12: Express Delivery and Growth Rates 2019-2023

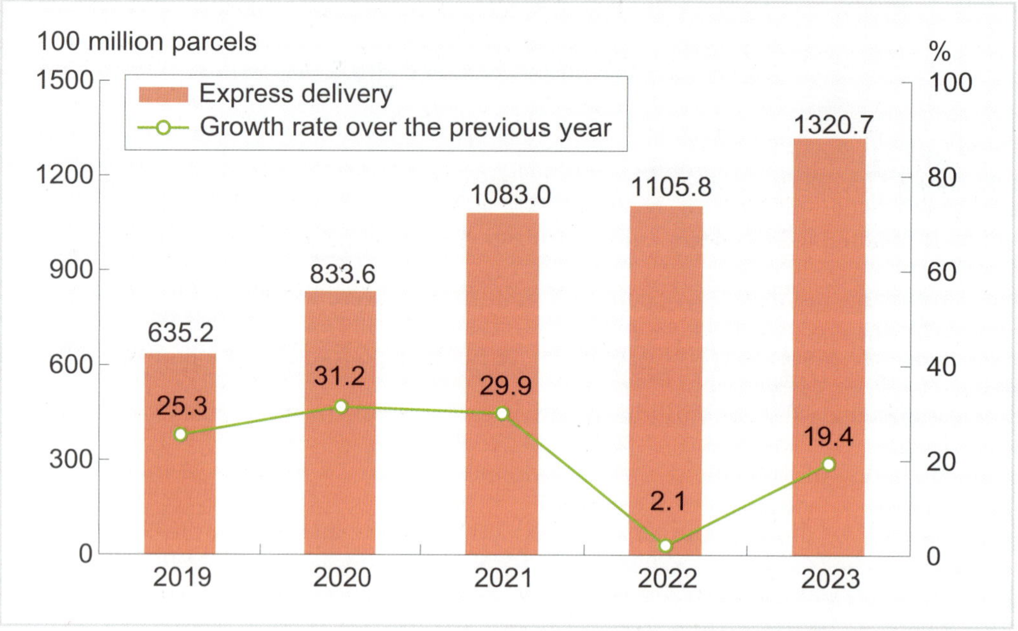

Figure 13: Year-end Number of Fixed Broadband Internet Users 2019-2023

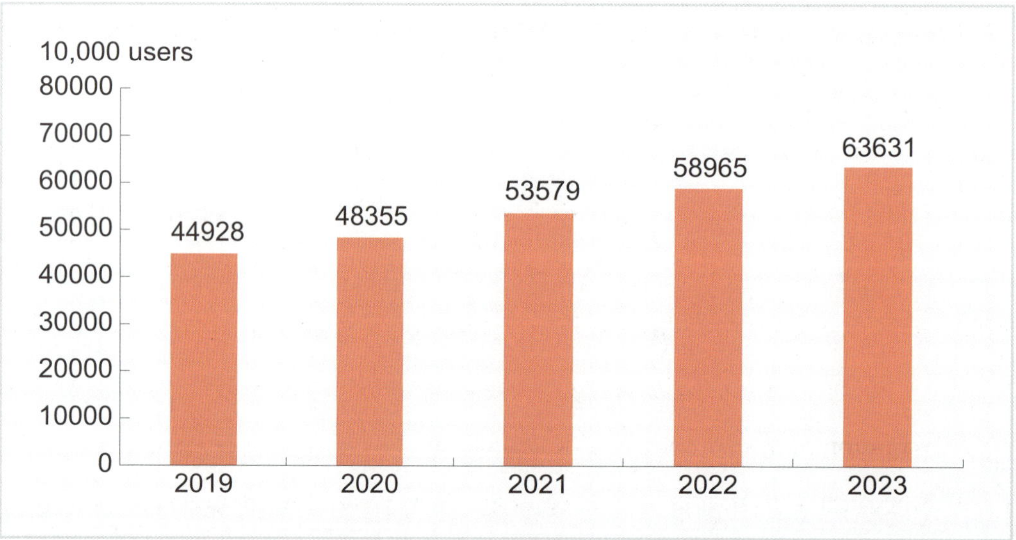

V. Domestic Trade

In 2023, the total retail sales of consumer goods reached 47,149.5 billion yuan, up by 7.2 percent over the previous year. An analysis on different areas showed that the retail sales of consumer goods in urban areas stood at 40,749.0 billion yuan, up by 7.1 percent, and that in rural areas reached 6,400.5 billion yuan, up by 8.0 percent. Grouped by consumption patterns, the retail sales of commodities were 41,860.5 billion yuan, up by 5.8 percent, and the income of catering industry was 5,289.0 billion yuan, up by 20.4 percent. The retail sales of services[36] increased by 20.0 percent over the previous year.

Figure 14: Total Retail Sales of Consumer Goods and Growth Rates 2019-2023

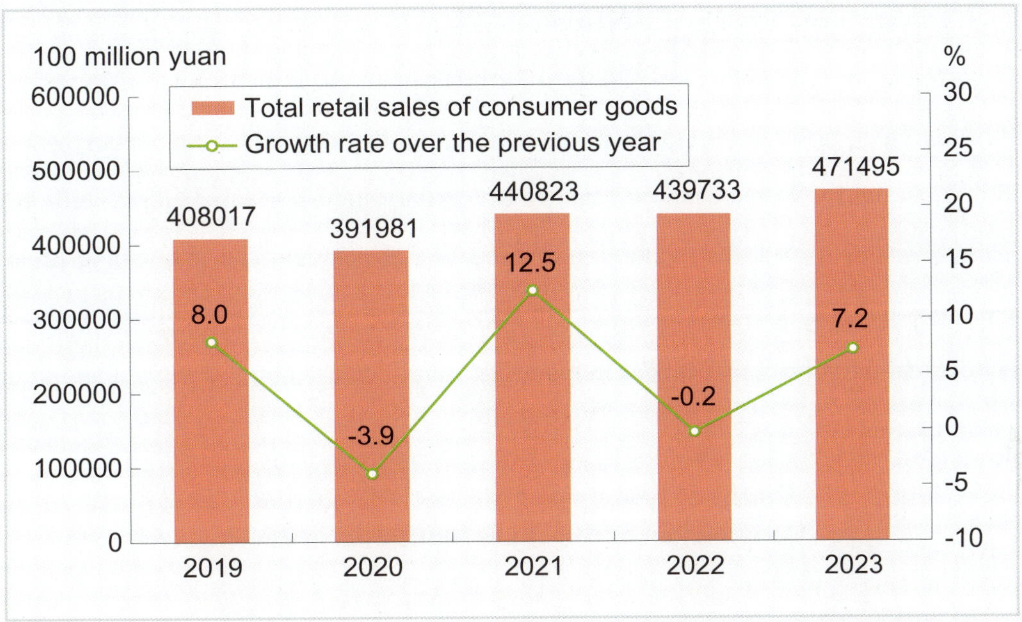

Of the total retail sales of commodities by enterprises above the designated size, the retail sales for grain, oil and food went up by 5.2 percent over the previous year; beverage up by 3.2 percent; tobacco and liquor up by 10.6 percent; clothes, shoes, hats and textiles up by 12.9 percent; cosmetics up by 5.1 percent; gold, silver and jewelry up by 13.3 percent; daily necessities up by 2.7 percent; household appliances and audio-video equipment up by 0.5 percent; traditional Chinese and western medicines up by 5.1 percent; cultural and office appliances down by 6.1 percent; furniture up by 2.8 percent; telecommunication equipment up by 7.0 percent; petroleum and petroleum products up by 6.6 percent; motor vehicles up by 5.9 percent; and building and decoration materials down by 7.8 percent.

In 2023, the online retail sales of physical goods were 13,017.4 billion yuan, up by 8.4 percent over the previous year on a comparable basis, accounting for 27.6 percent of the total retail sales of consumer goods.

VI. Investment in Fixed Assets

The total investment in fixed assets of the country in 2023 was 50,970.8 billion yuan, up by 2.8 percent

36. The retail sales of services refer to the total value of services directly provided by enterprises (establishments, self-employed units) to individuals and other units for non-production and non-operating purposes in the form of transactions. It aims to reflect the value of services with the nature of consumption sold by service providers in monetary terms, including the retail sales of services in transportation, accommodation, catering, education, health, sports, entertainment, and other fields.

over the previous year[37]. The investment in fixed assets (excluding rural households) was 50,303.6 billion yuan, up by 3.0 percent. Of the investment in fixed assets (excluding rural households), by regions[38], the investment in eastern areas was up by 4.4 percent, central areas up by 0.3 percent, western areas up by 0.1 percent, and northeastern areas down by 1.8 percent.

Of the investment in fixed assets (excluding rural households), the investment in the primary industry was 1,008.5 billion yuan, down by 0.1 percent over the previous year; that in the secondary industry was 16,213.6 billion yuan, up by 9.0 percent; and that in the tertiary industry was 33,081.5 billion yuan, up by 0.4 percent. The investment in infrastructure[39] increased by 5.9 percent. The investment in social sector[40] increased by 0.5 percent. The private investment in fixed assets[41] was 25,354.4 billion yuan, down by 0.4 percent; among which, the private investment in manufacturing increased by 9.4 percent and in infrastructure increased by 14.2 percent.

Figure 15: Shares of Investment in Fixed Assets (Excluding Rural Households) of the Three Industries in 2023

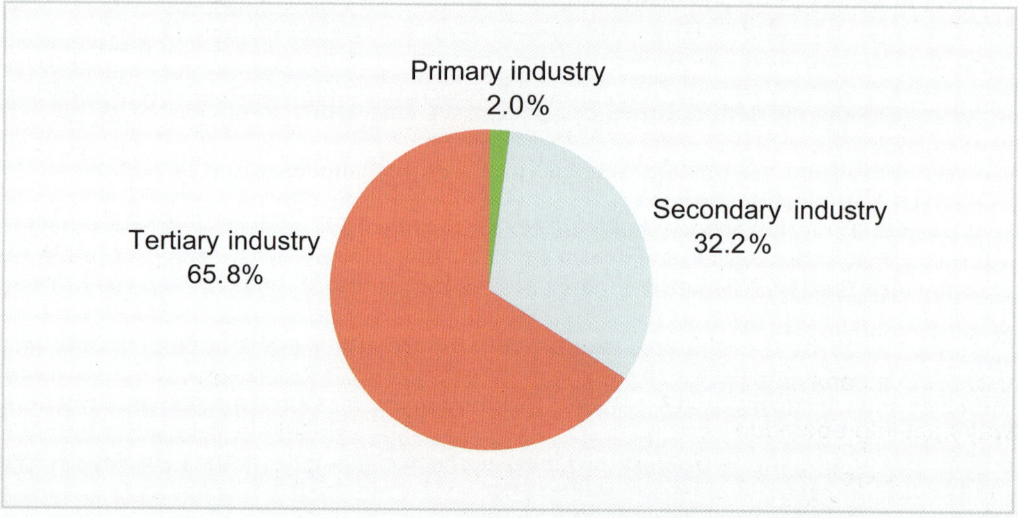

37. The growth rates of relevant indicators of investment in fixed assets were calculated on a comparable basis. Factors causing incomparability between the data of reporting period and the data released of the same period in the previous year made it impossible to calculate the growth rates directly. The main reasons were as below: ① The upfront land costs which should not be included as investment completed in the reporting period, as well as duplicated data across regions and industries were removed as data quality review and assessment methods were improved. ② Current assets and consumptive biological assets that were not within the statistical coverage of investment in fixed assets were removed in the review over the ongoing investment projects. ③ Problematic data were spotted and revised according to relevant rules as a result of statistical law enforcement.

38. See Note 20.

39. Investment in infrastructure includes investment in railway transportation, highway transportation, waterway transportation, civil aviation transportation, pipeline transportation, multi-modal transportation and forwarding agency, loading, unloading and delivery, postal service, telecommunication, radio, TV and satellite transmission, internet and related services, management of water conservancy, ecological conservation and environmental governance, and management of public facilities.

40. Investment in social sector includes investment in education, health and social services, culture, sports and recreation.

41. Private investment in fixed assets refers to investment in the construction or purchase of fixed assets by domestic collective, private and individual-owned enterprises and institutions or their holding enterprises (including absolute holding and relative holding enterprises).

Table 7: Growth Rates of Investment in Fixed Assets (Excluding Rural Households) by Sectors in 2023

Sector	Increase over 2022 (%)	Sector	Increase over 2022 (%)
Total	**3.0**	Financial Intermediation	-11.9
Agriculture, Forestry, Animal Husbandry and Fishery	1.2	Real Estate[42]	-8.1
Mining	2.1	Leasing and Business Services	9.9
Manufacturing	6.5	Scientific Research and Technical Services	18.1
Production and Supply of Electricity, Heat Power, Gas and Water	23.0	Water Conservancy, Environment and Public Facilities Management	0.1
Construction	22.5	Services to Households, Repair and Other Services	15.8
Wholesale and Retail Trades	-0.4	Education	2.8
Transport, Storage and Post	10.5	Health and Social Services	-3.8
Hotels and Catering Services	8.2	Culture, Sports and Entertainment	2.6
Information Transmission, Software and Information Technology Services	13.8	Public Management, Social Security and Social Organizations	-37.0

Table 8: Newly Increased Production and Operation Capacity through Fixed Assets Investment in 2023

Item	Unit	Volume
Newly increased alternating current transformer equipment with a capacity of over 220 kilovolts	10,000 kilovolt-amperes	25656
New railways put into operation	kilometer	3637
Of which: high-speed railways	kilometer	2776
Extended or new double-track railways put into operation	kilometer	3351
Electrified railways put into operation	kilometer	4463
Length of new and rebuilt highways	kilometer	7498
New throughput capacity of berths for over 10,000-tonnage ships	10,000 tons/year	32529
New civil transportation airports	-	5
New lines of optical-fiber cables	10,000 km	474

42. The investment in real estate includes the investment in real estate development, construction of buildings for own use, property management, intermediary services and other real estate investment.

In 2023, the investment in real estate development was 11,091.3 billion yuan, down by 9.6 percent over the previous year[43]. Of this total, the investment in residential buildings reached 8,382.0 billion yuan, a decrease of 9.3 percent, that in office buildings was 453.1 billion yuan, down by 9.4 percent, and that in buildings for commercial business was 805.5 billion yuan, down by 16.9 percent. In 2023, the floor space of newly built commercial buildings sold[44] was 1,117.35 million square meters. The floor space of second-hand housing online transactions[45] reached 708.82 million square meters. The floor space of newly built commercial buildings for sale was 672.95 million square meters at the end of 2023, among which the floor space of the commercial residential buildings for sale was 331.19 million square meters.

Table 9: Main Indicators for Real Estate Development and Sales and Growth Rates in 2023

Item	Unit	Volume	Increase over 2022 (%)
Investment in real estate development	100 million RMB	110913	-9.6
Of which: residential buildings	100 million RMB	83820	-9.3
Floor space of buildings under construction	10000 square meters	838364	-7.2
Of which: residential buildings	10000 square meters	589884	-7.7
Floor space of buildings newly started	10000 square meters	95376	-20.4
Of which: residential buildings	10000 square meters	69286	-20.9
Floor space of buildings completed	10000 square meters	99831	17.0
Of which: residential buildings	10000 square meters	72433	17.2
Floor space of newly built commercial buildings sold	10000 square meters	111735	-8.5
Of which: residential buildings	10000 square meters	94796	-8.2
Funds for investment this year of real estate development enterprises	100 million RMB	127459	-13.6
Of which: domestic loans	100 million RMB	15595	-9.9
individual mortgage	100 million RMB	21489	-9.1

43. The growth rates of indicators such as the investment in real estate development and the newly built commercial buildings sold were calculated on a comparable basis. Factors causing incomparability between the data of reporting period and the data released of the same period in the previous year made it impossible to calculate the growth rates directly. The main reasons were as below: ① Simple primary land development that didn't belong to the real estate development were removed in the review over the ongoing real estate development projects. ② Data that didn't belong to the sale of commercial buildings, such as transactions canceled and buildings mortgaged, were removed in the review over sales data of commercial buildings. ③ Problematic data were spotted and revised according to relevant rules as a result of statistical law enforcement.

44. The floor space of newly built commercial buildings sold refers to the total contract floor space of newly built commercial buildings sold by real estate development enterprises within the reporting period.

45. The floor space of second-hand housing online transactions refers to the total contract floor space of second-hand housing online transactions in urban areas within the reporting period.

In 2023, 1.59 million housing units were started to be rebuilt in rundown urban areas nationwide and 1.93 million were basically completed. There were 2.13 million units of government-subsidized rental housing that were started to be built or made available. Renovation began on 53.7 thousand old urban residential communities, benefiting 8.97 million households.

VII. Foreign Economic Relations

The total value of imports and exports of goods in 2023 reached 41,756.8 billion yuan, up by 0.2 percent over that of the previous year. Of this total, the value of goods exported was 23,772.6 billion yuan, up by 0.6 percent; the value of goods imported was 17,984.2 billion yuan, down by 0.3 percent. The surplus of trade in goods reached 5,788.3 billion yuan, up by 193.8 billion yuan over that of the previous year. The total value of imports and exports between China and countries along the Belt and Road[46] was 19,471.9 billion yuan, an increase of 2.8 percent over that of the previous year. Of this total, the value of goods exported was 10,731.4 billion yuan, up by 6.9 percent; the value of goods imported was 8,740.5 billion yuan, down by 1.9 percent. The total value of imports and exports between China and other Regional Comprehensive Economic Partnership (RCEP) member countries[47] was 12,596.7 billion yuan, down by 1.6 percent over that of the previous year. The total value of imports and exports by private enterprises was 22,360.1 billion yuan, up by 6.3 percent over that of the previous year, accounting for 53.5 percent of the total value of imports and exports.

Figure 16: Total Value of Imports and Exports of Goods 2019-2023

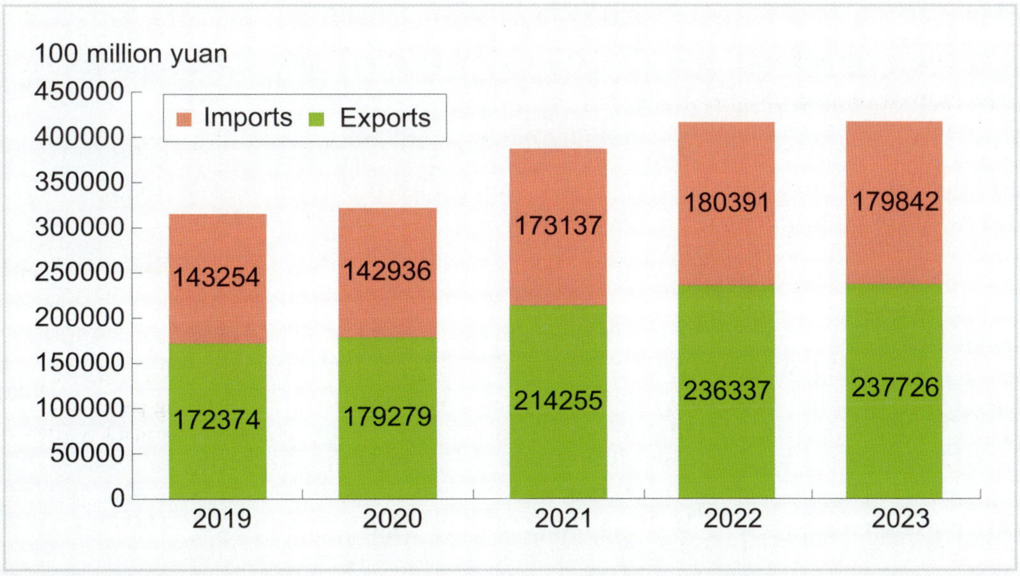

46. The Belt and Road refers to the Silk Road Economic Belt and the 21st Century Maritime Silk Road.

47. Other Regional Comprehensive Economic Partnership (RCEP) member countries include Indonesia, Malaysia, Philippines, Thailand, Singapore, Brunei, Cambodia, Laos, Myanmar, Vietnam, Japan, Republic of Korea, Australia and New Zealand.

Table 10: Total Value and Growth Rates of Imports and Exports of Goods in 2023

Item	Value (100 million yuan)	Increase over 2022 (%)
Total value of imports and exports of goods	**417568**	**0.2**
Exports	237726	0.6
Of which: General trade	153530	2.5
Processing trade	49062	-9.0
Of which: Mechanical and electronic products	139196	2.9
High & new technology products	59279	-5.8
Imports	179842	-0.3
Of which: General trade	117042	1.3
Processing trade	27061	-11.3
Of which: Mechanical and electronic products	65363	-5.5
High & new technology products	47916	-5.2
Trade surplus in goods	**57883**	**3.5**

Table 11: Main Export Commodities in Volume and Value and the Growth Rates in 2023

Item	Unit	Volume	Increase over 2022 (%)	Value (100 million yuan)	Increase over 2022 (%)
Rolled steel	10000 tons	9026	36.2	5929	-3.4
Textile yarns and textile articles	—	—	—	9454	-3.1
Clothes and clothing accessories	—	—	—	11206	-2.8
Footwear	10000 pairs	891424	-2.5	3470	-8.0
Furniture and parts	—	—	—	4517	0.2
Luggage and similar containers	10000 tons	331	13.5	2512	9.3
Toys	—	—	—	2858	-7.4
Plastic articles	—	—	—	7090	1.4
Integrated circuits	100 million pieces	2678	-1.8	9568	-5.0
Automatic data processing machines and components	—	—	—	13187	-15.8
Mobile phones	10000 sets	80213	-2.0	9797	2.9
Containers	10000 units	231	-27.9	581	-39.8
Liquid crystal display modules	10000 units	168929	2.9	1873	3.8
Motor vehicles (including chassis)	10000 sets	522	57.4	7165	76.8

Table 12: Main Import Commodities in Volume and Value and the Growth Rates in 2023

Item	Unit	Volume	Increase over 2022 (%)	Value (100 million yuan)	Increase over 2022 (%)
Soybean	10000 tons	9941	11.4	4199	4.8
Edible vegetable oil	10000 tons	981	51.4	734	21.1
Iron ore and concentrate	10000 tons	117906	6.6	9418	11.2
Coal and lignite	10000 tons	47442	61.8	3723	30.2
Crude oil	10000 tons	56399	11.0	23733	-2.6
Petroleum products refined	10000 tons	4769	80.3	1965	50.0
Natural gas	10000 tons	11997	9.9	4523	-3.4
Plastics in primary forms	10000 tons	2960	-3.2	3182	-14.8
Paper pulp	10000 tons	3666	25.7	1665	11.6
Rolled steel	10000 tons	765	-27.6	891	-21.5
Unwrought copper and its alloys	10000 tons	550	-6.3	3356	-6.9
Integrated circuits	100 million pieces	4796	-10.8	24591	-10.6
Motor vehicles (including chassis)	10000 sets	80	-8.9	3321	-5.8

Table 13: Imports and Exports of Goods by Major Countries and Regions, the Growth Rates and Proportions in 2023

Country or region	Exports (100 million yuan)	Increase over 2022 (%)	Proportion of the total (%)	Imports (100 million yuan)	Increase over 2022 (%)	Proportion of the total (%)
ASEAN	36817	0.0	15.5	27309	0.4	15.2
European Union	35226	-5.3	14.8	19833	4.6	11.0
United States	35198	-8.1	14.8	11528	-1.8	6.4
Japan	11076	-3.5	4.7	11309	-7.9	6.3
Republic of Korea	10467	-2.2	4.4	11381	-13.9	6.3
Hong Kong, China	19333	-1.3	8.1	958	84.3	0.5
Taiwan, China	4819	-11.1	2.0	14033	-10.5	7.8
Russia	7823	53.9	3.3	9093	18.6	5.1
Brazil	4159	1.0	1.7	8625	18.4	4.8
India	8279	6.5	3.5	1301	12.2	0.7
South Africa	1661	4.4	0.7	2245	3.7	1.2

The total value of imports and exports of services in 2023 was 6,575.4 billion yuan, up by 10.0 percent over that of the previous year. The export value of services was 2,685.7 billion yuan, down by 5.8 percent. The import value of services was 3,889.8 billion yuan, up by 24.4 percent. The trade deficit in imports and exports of services was 1,204.1 billion yuan.

The year 2023 witnessed the establishment of 53,766 enterprises with foreign direct investment, up by 39.7 percent over that of the previous year, and the foreign direct investment actually utilized totaled 1,133.9 billion yuan, down by 8.0 percent, or 163.3 billion US dollars, down by 13.7 percent. Specifically, there were 13,649 newly established enterprises with direct investment from countries along the Belt and Road (including the investment in China via free ports), up by 82.7 percent; and the foreign capital directly invested in China reached 122.1 billion yuan, down by 11.4 percent, or 17.6 billion US dollars, down by 16.7 percent. In 2023, the foreign investment actually utilized by high technology industry reached 423.3 billion yuan, down by 4.9 percent, or 61.0 billion US dollars, down by 10.8 percent.

Table 14: Total Value of Foreign Direct Investment and the Growth Rates in 2023

Sector	Enterprises	Increase over 2022 (%)	Actually Utilized Value (100 million yuan)	Increase over 2022 (%)
Total	**53766**	**39.7**	**11339**	**-8.0**
Of which: Agriculture, Forestry, Animal Husbandry and Fishery	418	-0.5	51	-36.8
Manufacturing	3624	1.5	3179	-1.8
Production and Supply of Electricity, Heat Power, Gas and Water	568	8.6	319	15.6
Transport, Storage and Post	867	44.0	149	-57.2
Information Transmission, Software and Information Technology Services	3764	23.0	1134	-26.7
Wholesale and Retail	18010	65.3	690	-28.2
Real Estate	684	17.7	810	-11.4
Leasing and Business Services	10673	42.8	1819	-15.4
Services to Households, Repair and Other Services	726	76.6	34	77.7

In 2023, the non-financial outbound direct investment reached 917.0 billion yuan, up by 16.7 percent over that of the previous year, or 130.1 billion US dollars, up by 11.4 percent. Of this total, that to countries along the Belt and Road reached 224.1 billion yuan, up by 28.4 percent, or 31.8 billion US dollars, up by 22.6 percent.

Table 15: Total Value and Growth Rates of Non-financial Outbound Direct Investment in 2023

Sector	Value (100 million US dollars)	Increase over 2022 (%)
Total	**1301**	**11.4**
Of which: Agriculture, Forestry, Animal Husbandry and Fishery	8	-3.6
Mining	70	39.0
Manufacturing	279	29.0
Production and Supply of Electricity, Heat Power, Gas and Water	31	-12.5
Construction	67	5.1
Wholesale and Retail	292	38.6
Transport, Storage and Post	65	42.3
Information Transmission, Software and Information Technology Services	49	-10.9
Real Estate	10	-57.4
Leasing and Business Services	337	-13.0

In 2023, the accomplished business revenue through contracted overseas engineering projects was 1,133.9 billion yuan, up by 8.8 percent over that of the previous year, or 160.9 billion US dollars, up by 3.8 percent. Specifically, the accomplished business revenue from countries along the Belt and Road was 132.1 billion US dollars, up by 4.8 percent, accounting for 82.1 percent of the accomplished business revenue through contracted overseas engineering projects. The number of labor forces sent abroad through overseas labor contracts was 0.35 million.

VIII. Finance and Financial Intermediation

The national general public budget revenue reached 21,678.4 billion yuan in 2023, up by 6.4 percent over that of the previous year, of which tax revenue amounted to 18,112.9 billion yuan, up by 8.7 percent. The national general public budget expenditure reached 27,457.4 billion yuan, up by 5.4 percent over that of the previous year. The newly added tax refunds, as well as tax and fee cuts and deferrals exceeded 2.2 trillion yuan in 2023.

Figure 17: National General Public Budget Revenue 2019-2023

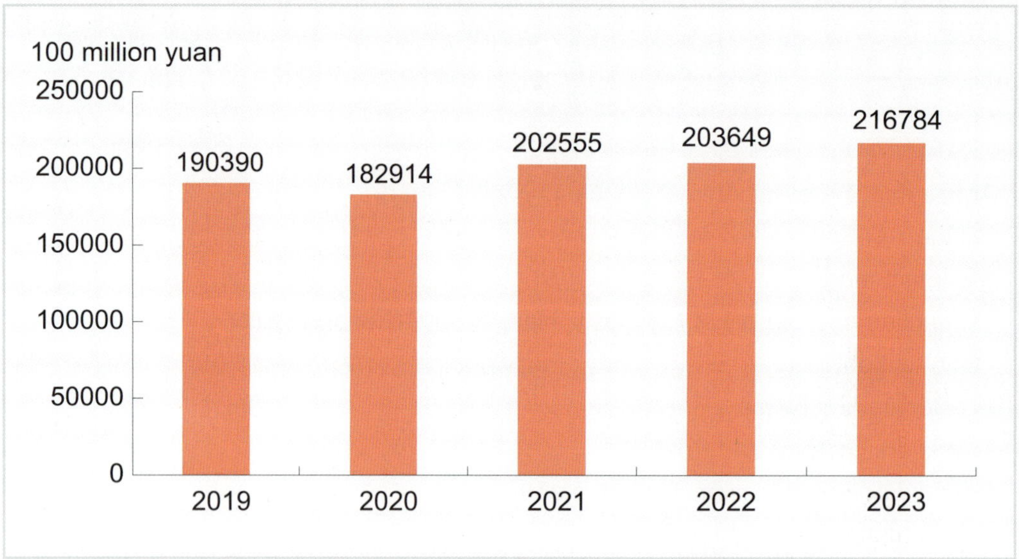

Note: Data for general public budget revenue from 2019 to 2022 as shown in the figure were final accounts and that of 2023 was the executive accounts.

By the end of 2023, money supply of broad sense (M_2) was 292.3 trillion yuan, an increase of 9.7 percent over that by the end of the previous year. Money supply of narrow sense (M_1) was 68.1 trillion yuan, up by 1.3 percent. Cash in circulation (M_0) was 11.3 trillion yuan, up by 8.3 percent.

In 2023, the aggregate financing to the real economy (AFRE) (flow)[48] reached 35.6 trillion yuan, or 3.4 trillion yuan more than that in 2022 on a comparable basis. The AFRE (stock)[49] totaled 378.1 trillion yuan at the end of 2023, up by 9.5 percent over that at the end of 2022 on a comparable basis. Specifically, loans granted to the real economy in Renminbi stood at 235.5 trillion yuan, up by 10.4 percent. Savings deposit in Renminbi and foreign currencies in all items of financial institutions totaled 289.9 trillion yuan at the end of 2023, an increase of 25.4 trillion yuan compared with that at the beginning of the year. Of this total, the savings deposit in Renminbi stood at 284.3 trillion yuan, an increase of 25.7 trillion yuan. Loans in Renminbi and foreign currencies in all items of financial institutions reached 242.2 trillion yuan, an increase of 22.2 trillion yuan. Of this total, loans in Renminbi were 237.6 trillion yuan, an increase of 22.7 trillion yuan. Inclusive loans to micro and small businesses in Renminbi[50] reached 29.4 trillion yuan, an increase of 5.6

48. The AFRE (flow) refers to the total volume of financing provided by the financial system to the real economy within a certain period of time.

49. The AFRE (stock) refers to the outstanding financing provided by the financial system to the real economy at the end of a period of time (a month, a quarter or a year).

50. Inclusive loans to micro and small businesses include loans to micro and small businesses with single-client credit line under 10 million yuan, operating loans to self-employed businesses and owners of micro and small businesses.

trillion yuan. Medium and long-term loans to the manufacturing sector in Renminbi reached 12.2 trillion yuan, an increase of 3.1 trillion yuan.

Table 16: Savings Deposit and Loans in RMB and Foreign Currencies in All Financial Institutions and the Growth Rates at the End of 2023

Item	Year-end figure (100 million yuan)	Increase over 2022 (%)
Savings deposit	**2899132**	**9.6**
Domestic households	1378765	13.8
Deposits in RMB	1369895	13.8
Domestic non-financial enterprises	817959	4.9
Loans	**2422396**	**10.1**
Domestic short-term loans	623037	10.2
Domestic medium- and long-term loans	1591965	11.3

Loans in Renminbi from rural financial institutions (rural credit cooperatives, rural cooperation banks and rural commercial banks) totaled 29,358.4 billion yuan by the end of 2023, an increase of 2,636.3 billion yuan as compared with that at the beginning of the year. Loans in Renminbi for consumption use from all financial institutions totaled 57,943.8 billion yuan, an increase of 1,099.2 billion yuan. Of the total, household short-term consumption loans totaled 10,354.1 billion yuan, an increase of 507.8 billion yuan, and household medium and long-term consumption loans reached 47,589.7 billion yuan, an increase of 591.4 billion yuan.

Funds raised through A-shares issued on Shanghai and Shenzhen Stock Exchanges[51] amounted to 1,073.4 billion yuan in 2023, a decrease of 437.5 billion yuan from the previous year. A total of 236 new A-shares issued on Shanghai and Shenzhen Stock Exchanges raised 341.8 billion yuan worth of capital altogether, down by 228.6 billion yuan over that of the previous year. Of the total, 67 shares on the Science and Technology Innovation Board raised 143.9 billion yuan; refinancing of A-shares on Shanghai and Shenzhen Stock Exchanges (including public newly issued, targeted placement, right issued, preferred stock and exchanged convertible bonds) raised 731.6 billion yuan, a decrease of 208.9 billion yuan over that of the previous year. Funds raised through Beijing Stock Exchanges[52] reached 14.6 billion yuan with 77 shares publicly issued. Market entities raised 13,067.7 billion yuan through issuing bonds (including corporate

51. Funds raised through Shanghai and Shenzhen Stock Exchanges are calculated by the money raised on the listing date, and the funds raised include the actual exchanged convertible bonds, which were 93.4 billion yuan in 2022 and 83.2 billion yuan in 2023.
52. Funds raised through Beijing Stock Exchanges are calculated by the money raised on the listing date.

bonds, asset-backed securities, national and local government bonds and policy bank bonds) on Shanghai, Shenzhen and Beijing Stock Exchanges. Specifically, 40 Real Estate Investment Trust Funds (REITs) in infrastructure sector were issued and listed on Shanghai and Shenzhen Stock Exchanges, raising 91.4 billion yuan. There were 6,241 companies listed on National Equities Exchange and Quotations[53] and 18.0 billion yuan raised by listed companies in 2023.

In 2023, the issuance of corporate credit bonds[54] reached 13.8 trillion yuan, an increase of 0.1 trillion yuan over that of the previous year.

The premium of primary insurance received by the insurance companies[55] totaled 5,124.7 billion yuan in 2023, up by 9.1 percent over that of the previous year. Of this total, life insurance premium of primary insurance amounted to 2,764.6 billion yuan, health and casualty insurance premium of primary insurance 999.3 billion yuan, and property insurance premium of primary insurance 1,360.7 billion yuan. An indemnity worth of 1,888.3 billion yuan was paid, of which, life insurance indemnity was 550.5 billion yuan, health and casualty insurance indemnity 420.7 billion yuan, and property insurance indemnity 917.1 billion yuan.

IX. Households Income and Consumption and Social Security

In 2023, the per capita disposable income nationwide was 39,218 yuan, an increase of 6.3 percent over that of the previous year or a real increase of 6.1 percent after deducting price factors. The median[56] of per capita disposable income nationwide was 33,036 yuan, up by 5.3 percent. In terms of permanent residence, the per capita disposable income of urban households was 51,821 yuan, up by 5.1 percent over that of 2022, or a real growth of 4.8 percent after deducting price factors. The median of per capita disposable income of urban households was 47,122 yuan, up by 4.4 percent. The per capita disposable income of rural households was 21,691 yuan, up by 7.7 percent over that of the previous year, or 7.6 percent in real terms after deducting price factors. The median of per capita disposable income of rural households was 18,748 yuan, up by 5.7 percent. The urban-rural per capita disposable income ratio was 2.39, narrowed by 0.06 over that of the

53. National Equities Exchange and Quotations is a national securities exchange established upon approval by the State Council in 2012. Preferred stocks were excluded from funds raised by listed companies in National Equities Exchange and Quotations. Funds raised by shares are calculated by the disclosure date of the issuance report.

54. Corporate credit bonds include debt financing instruments issued by non-financial businesses, enterprise bonds, corporate bonds and convertible bonds.

55. The premium of primary insurance received by the insurance companies refers to the premium income from primary insurance contracts confirmed by the insurance companies.

56. The median of per capita disposable income refers to the per capita income of household lied in the middle of all surveyed households which are ranked from low to high (or high to low) based on per capita disposable income level.

previous year. Grouped by income quintile[57], the per capita disposable income of low-income group reached 9,215 yuan, the lower-middle-income group 20,442 yuan, the middle-income group 32,195 yuan, the upper-middle-income group 50,220 yuan and the high-income group 95,055 yuan. The per capita monthly income of migrant workers was 4,780 yuan, increased by 3.6 percent over that of the previous year. In 2023, the per capita disposable income of rural households from counties lifted out of poverty[58] was 16,396 yuan, up by 8.5 percent over that of 2022, or a real growth of 8.4 percent after deducting price factors.

The national per capita consumption expenditure was 26,796 yuan, up by 9.2 percent over that of the previous year, or a real increase of 9.0 percent after deducting price factors. Specifically, the per capita consumption expenditure on services[59] totaled 12,114 yuan, up by 14.4 percent over that of the previous year, accounting for 45.2 percent of the per capita consumption expenditure. In terms of permanent residence, the per capita consumption expenditure of urban households was 32,994 yuan, up by 8.6 percent, or up by 8.3 percent in real terms after deducting price factors. The per capita consumption expenditure of rural households was 18,175 yuan, up by 9.3 percent, or a real increase of 9.2 percent after deducting price factors. The national Engel's Coefficient stood at 29.8 percent, with that of urban and rural households standing at 28.8 percent and 32.4 percent respectively.

Figure 18: National Per Capita Disposable Income and the Growth Rates 2019-2023

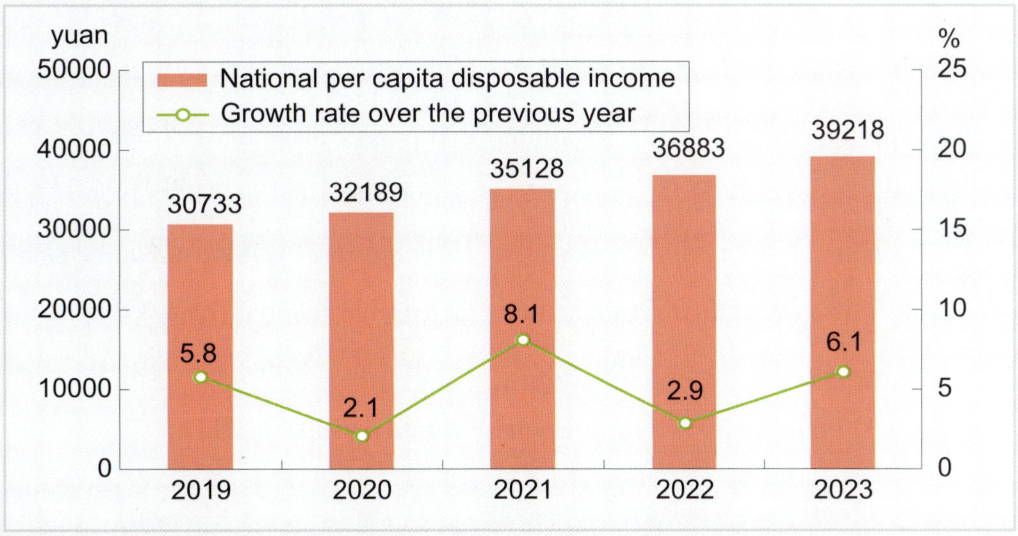

57. The income quintile refers to the five equal partitions of all surveyed households, who are ranked from low to high based on per capita income level. The top 20 percent with the highest income are classified as high-income group, and the other four levels are upper-middle-income group, middle-income group, lower-middle-income group and low-income group.

58. Counties lifted out of poverty include 832 key counties under the national poverty alleviation and development program and counties in contiguous poor areas as well as 7 cities and counties in Aksu prefecture, Xinjiang.

59. The consumption expenditure on services refers to the spending by households on services for daily lives including catering, clothing and footwear processing, housing, family, transportation and telecommunication, education, culture and recreation, medical services and others.

Figure 19: National Per Capita Consumption Expenditure and Composition in 2023

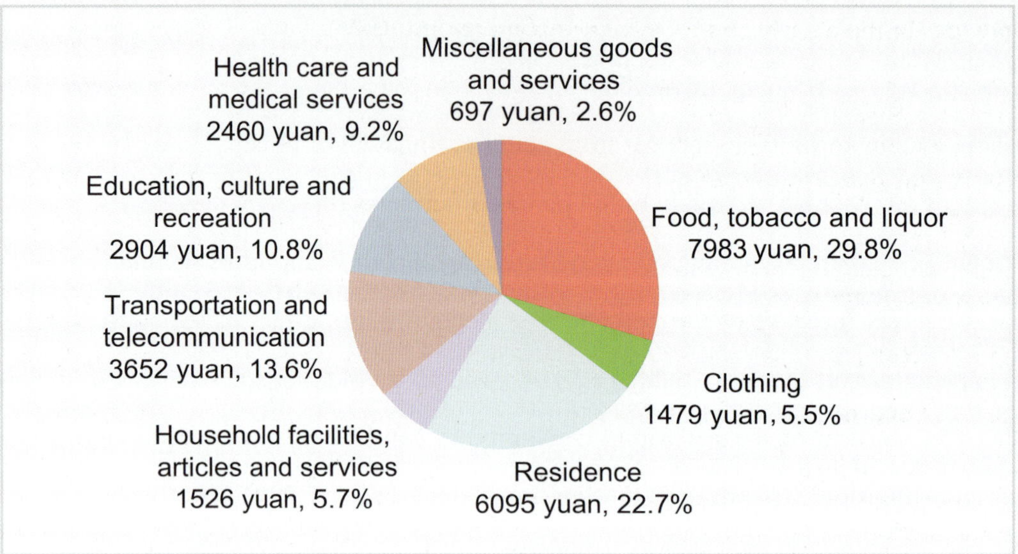

By the end of 2023, a total of 521.21 million people participated in the basic endowment insurance program for urban workers, an increase of 17.66 million over that by the end of 2022. A total of 545.22 million people participated in basic endowment insurance program for urban and rural residents, a decrease of 4.30 million. A total of 1,333.87 million people participated in basic medical insurance program[60]. Of this total, 370.94 million people participated in the program for workers, and 962.93 million people participated in the program for urban and rural residents. A total of 243.73 million people participated in unemployment insurance program, an increase of 5.66 million. The number of people receiving unemployment insurance payment stood at 3.52 million. A total of 301.70 million people participated in work-related injury insurance, an increase of 10.54 million. A total of 249.07 million people participated in maternity insurance programs. By the end of 2023, minimum living allowances were granted to 6.64 million urban residents and 33.99 million rural residents, 4.35 million rural residents living in extreme poverty[61] received relief and assistance and 7.42 million person-times of temporary assistance[62] were provided. National pensions and subsidies were regularly provided to 8.34 million ex-servicemen and other entitled people in 2023.

By the end of 2023, there were altogether 44 thousand social welfare institutions providing

60. Participants in basic medical insurance program for the year 2023 had the duplicated participation removed.

61. Rural residents living in extreme poverty refer to the aged, the disabled and the minor under 16 years of age in rural areas who have no ability to work, no sources of income and no statutory obligors to provide for them, bring them up or support them, or whose statutory obligors have no ability to fulfill their obligations.

62. Temporary assistance refers to emergent and transitional assistance provided by the government to families or individuals who experience hardships because of emergencies, unexpected harm, major diseases or other unusual factors and are not covered by other forms of social assistance programs or still suffer hardships after receiving other social assistance programs.

accommodation, of which 41 thousand were elderly care institutions and 971 were institutions for child welfare, assistance and protection. The social welfare institutions provided 8.463 million beds[63], of which 8.201 million were for the elderly and 98 thousand were for children.

X. Science & Technology and Education

Expenditures on research and experimental development activities (R&D) were 3,327.8 billion yuan in 2023, up by 8.1 percent over that of 2022, accounting for 2.64 percent of GDP. Of this total, 221.2 billion yuan was used for basic research programs, up by 9.3 percent over that of 2022, accounting for 6.65 percent of expenditures on R&D. A total of 52.5 thousand projects were financed by the National Natural Science Foundation. By the end of 2023, there were altogether 207 national engineering research centers included into the new sequence management and 1,798 state-level enterprise technology centers. The National Fund for Technology Transfer and Commercialization established 36 sub-funds, with a total funding of 62.4 billion yuan. There were 1,606 state-level technology business incubators[64], and 2,376 national mass makerspaces[65]. A total of 921 thousand invention patents were authorized, up by 15.3 percent over that of the previous year. The number of PCT patent applications accepted[66] was 74 thousand. By the end of 2023, the number of valid invention patents was 4.991 million, up by 18.5 percent over that by the end of 2022. The number of high-value invention patents per 10,000 people[67] was 11.8. Trademark registration totaled 4.383 million, down by 29.0 percent over that of the previous year. A total of 0.95 million technology contracts were signed with 6,147.6 billion yuan worth of contracted technology transactions, up by 28.6 percent over that of the previous year. The proportion of citizens with scientific literacy[68] in China reached 14.14 percent.

---

63. The beds provided by social welfare institutions include beds provided by adoption agencies, aid agencies and community agencies.

64. The state-level technology business incubators are technology-based business startup service providers consistent with the Administrative Measures for Technology Business Incubators that provide physical space, shared facilities and professional services with the mission of advancing transformation of technological achievements, cultivating technological enterprises and fostering the entrepreneurial spirit. They should be approved and accredited by the Ministry of Science and Technology.

65. The national mass makerspaces are new service platform for entrepreneurship and innovation that are in conformity with the Guidelines on Developing Mass Makerspaces and are reviewed and registered by the Ministry of Science and Technology in accordance with the Provisional Registration Regulations on National Mass Makerspaces.

66. The number of PCT patent applications accepted refers to the number of PCT patent application accepted by the State Intellectual Property Office which acts as the receiving office of PCT patent application. PCT is the abbreviation of Patent Cooperation Treaty, which is a treaty for international cooperation in the field of patents.

67. The number of high-value invention patents per 10,000 people refers to the number of valid invention patents owned per 10,000 national residents which are authorized by the China National Intellectual Property Administration and satisfy any of the following conditions: invention patents for strategic emerging industries; invention patents having corresponding foreign patents; invention patents maintained more than 10 years; invention patents with a relatively high pledge financing amount; and invention patents that won the National Science and Technology Award and the China Patent Award.

68. Citizens with scientific literacy refer to citizens carrying out scientific spirit, spreading scientific philosophy, mastering basic scientific methods and scientific knowledge, and able to apply them to analysis and problem solving. The proportion of citizens with scientific literacy was obtained from the sample survey for citizens aged from 18 to 69.

Figure 20: Expenditure on Research and Experimental Development Activities (R&D) and the Growth Rates 2019-2023

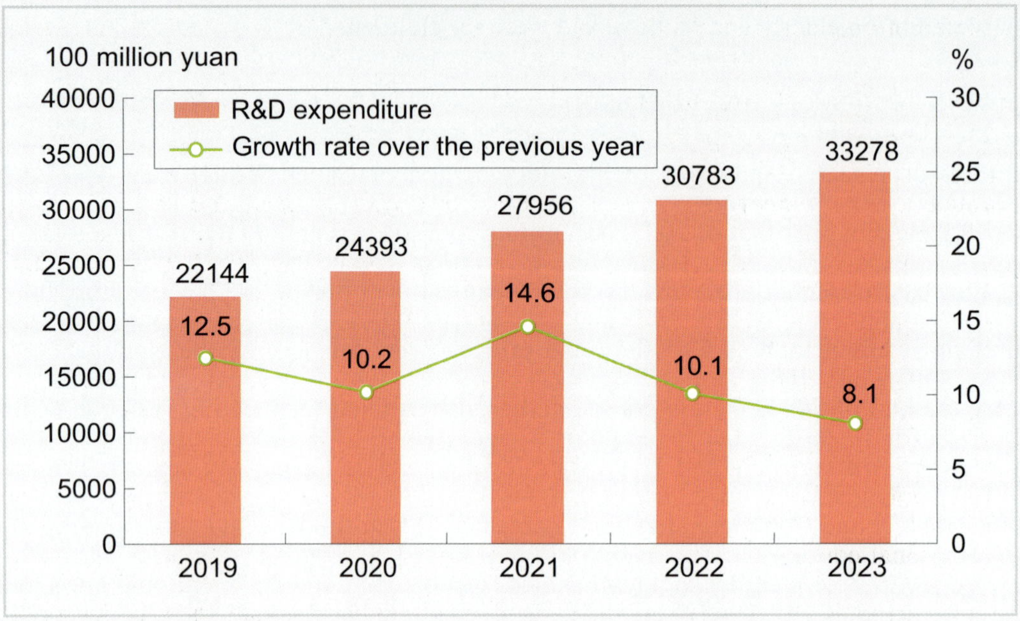

Table 17: Number of Patents Authorized and Valid Patents in 2023

Item	Patents (10,000)	Increase over 2022 (%)
Number of invention patents authorized	92.1	15.3
Of which: domestic	81.3	18.0
Number of utility model patents authorized	209.0	-25.5
Number of appearance design patents authorized	63.8	-11.5
Number of valid invention patents at the end of the year	499.1	18.5
Of which: domestic	401.5	22.4
Number of valid utility model patents at the end of the year	1212.9	11.9
Number of valid appearance design patents at the end of the year	323.4	14.2

The year 2023 saw a total of 66 successful space launches. The successive launches of the Tianzhou 6, Shenzhou 16 and Shenzhou 17 led China's space station to usher in a new phase of application and development. The world's first liquid oxygen-methane carrier rocket, ZQ-2 Y2, blasted off successfully. The Jiuzhang 3.0 quantum computer prototype was successfully developed. The experimental advanced superconducting tokamak (EAST) achieved a steady-state high confinement plasma operation for 403 seconds. The world's first fourth-generation high temperature gas-cooled reactor nuclear power plant has officially gone into commercial operation. The world's first 16-megawatt ultra-large-capacity offshore wind turbine was successfully connected to the grid and began generating electricity. China's C919 jetliner officially went into commercial operation. China's first domestically-built large cruise ship completed its first sea trial. The deep-sea manned submersible Fendouzhe completed its deep-diving mission.

By the end of 2023, there were altogether 877 national quality inspection centers. There were 1,242 agencies for product quality, management system and service certification which certified accumulatively 1.02 million enterprises. A total of 2,902 national standards were developed or revised in the year, including 1,708 new standards. The qualification rate of manufactured products[69] reached 93.65 percent.

In 2023, graduate institutes enrolled 3.883 million students with 1.302 million entrants and 1.015 million graduates. Total enrollment in undergraduate programs in regular and vocational higher education institutes[70] was 37.750 million with 10.422 million entrants and 10.470 million graduates. The enrollment in secondary vocational education[71] was 17.379 million, including 6.165 million entrants, and 5.371 million graduates. Regular senior secondary schools had 28.036 million enrolled students, including 9.678 million entrants, and 8.604 million graduates. Students enrolled in junior secondary schools totaled 52.437 million, including 17.546 million entrants, and 16.236 million graduates. The country had a primary education enrollment of 108.360 million, including 18.779 million entrants, and 17.635 million graduates. There were 0.912 million students enrolled in special education schools, with 0.155 million entrants and 0.173 million graduates. Kindergartens accommodated 40.930 million children. The number of students who graduated from compulsory education reached 95.7 percent of the total enrollment, and the gross enrollment ratio for senior secondary education reached 91.8 percent.

69. The qualification rate of manufactured products is the ratio of the samples that have passed the sampling quality test, the process of which follows certain methods, procedure and standard, to the total amount of the sampled products. The survey samples cover 29 sectors of the manufacturing industry.

70. Regular and vocational higher education institutes include regular universities, vocational undergraduate education and higher vocational colleges.

71. Secondary vocational education includes regular specialized secondary schools, adult specialized secondary schools, vocational high schools and skilled workers schools.

Figure 21: Entrants in Education 2019-2023

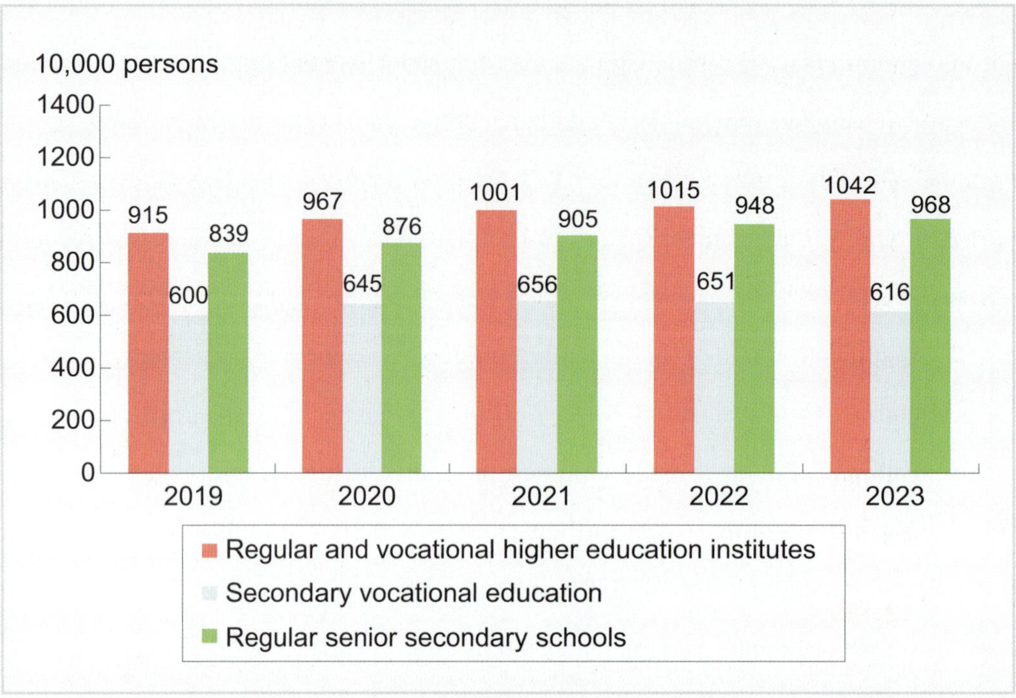

XI. Culture and Tourism, Public Health and Sports

By the end of 2023, there were 1,893 art-performing groups affiliated to government culture and tourism departments throughout China. A total of 3,309 public libraries received[72] 1,126.68 million person-times of visits. There were 3,508 cultural centers. Subscribers to cable television programs numbered 202 million, among which 193 million subscribed to digital cable television programs. By the end of 2023, radio broadcasting and television broadcasting coverage rates were 99.7 percent and 99.8 percent respectively. A total of 4,632 episodes of 156 TV series and 93,811 minutes of TV cartoons were produced in 2023. The country developed 792 feature movies and 179 popular science movies, documentaries, animation and special movies[73]. A total of 25.8 billion copies of newspapers and 1.8 billion copies of magazines were issued, and 11.9 billion copies of books were published. The average number of books possessed per person[74] was 8.40 copies. By the end of the year, there were 4,154 archives in China and 238.27 million files were made accessible to the public. The business revenue of enterprises above the designated size engaged in culture and related industries reached 12,951.5 billion yuan, up by 8.2 percent over that of the previous year

72. The people received by the public libraries refer to the number of people who visit libraries and use library services in the year, including borrowing and reading books, consultation and attending readers' programs.

73. Special movies refer to those using different display modes in terms of projection techniques, equipment and program as compared with the ordinary cinemas, such as IMAX movies, 3D movies, 4D movies, multidimensional movies and full dome movies.

74. The average number of books possessed per person refers to the average number of books published in the year that can be possessed per person in China.

on a comparable basis.

In 2023, a total of 4.89 billion domestic trips were made, up by 93.3 percent over that of the previous year. Of this total, the number of trips made by urban residents was 3.76 billion, an increase of 94.9 percent; and the number of trips made by rural residents was 1.13 billion, an increase of 88.5 percent. The expenditure of domestic tourists was 4,913.3 billion yuan, an increase of 140.3 percent. Of this total, tourists from urban areas spent 4,178.1 billion yuan, an increase of 147.5 percent; and tourists from rural areas spent 735.3 billion yuan, an increase of 106.4 percent. The number of inbound visits to China totaled 82.03 million. Of this total, 13.78 million were made by foreigners and 68.24 million by Chinese compatriots from Hong Kong, Macao and Taiwan. The expenditures of inbound visitors to China totaled 53.0 billion US dollars. The number of China's outbound visits totaled 100.96 million. Of this total, 96.84 million were private visits and 77.04 million were to Hong Kong, Macao and Taiwan.

Figure 22: Person-times of Domestic Tourists and the Growth Rates 2019-2023

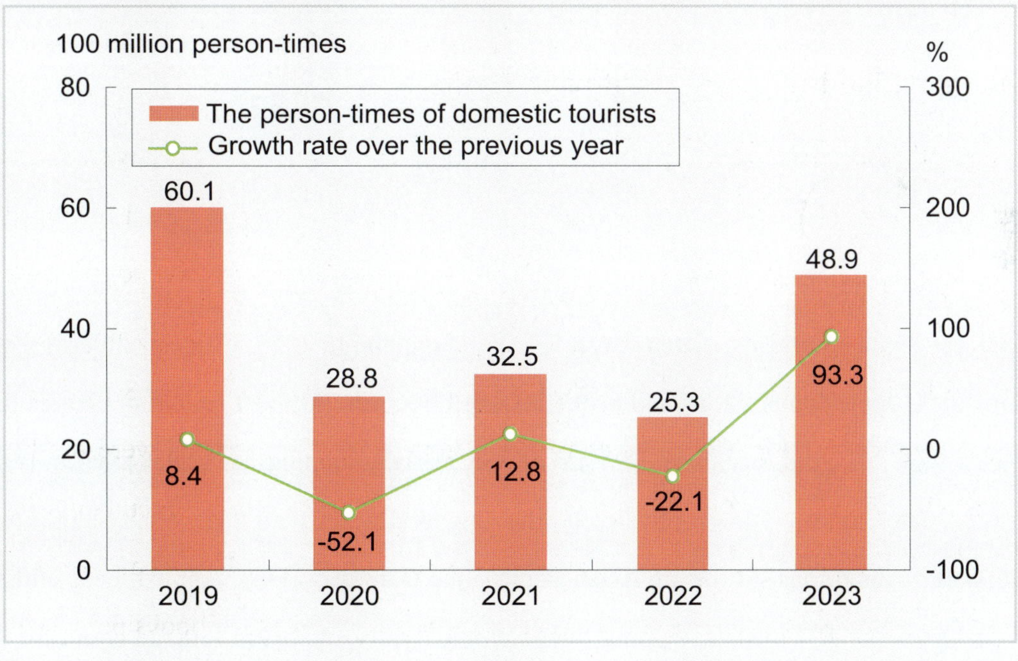

By the end of 2023, there were 1.071 million medical and health institutions in China, including 39 thousand hospitals. Of all the hospitals, 12 thousand were public, and 27 thousand were private. Of the 1.016 million medical and health institutions at grass-root level, 34 thousand were town and township health centers, 37 thousand community health service centers, 362 thousand clinics and 583 thousand village clinics. Of the 12 thousand professional public health institutions, 3,426 were disease control and prevention centers and 2,791 were health monitoring institutions. By the end of 2023, there were 12.47 million medical technical personnel in China, including 4.78 million licensed doctors and licensed assistant doctors and 5.63 million registered nurses. The medical and health institutions in China had 10.20 million beds, of which hospitals had 8.00 million and township health centers had 1.51 million. The total number of medical visits[75] and hospital discharges[76] in 2023 reached 9.56 billion and 0.3 billion respectively.

Figure 23: Year-end Number of Medical Technical Personnel 2019-2023

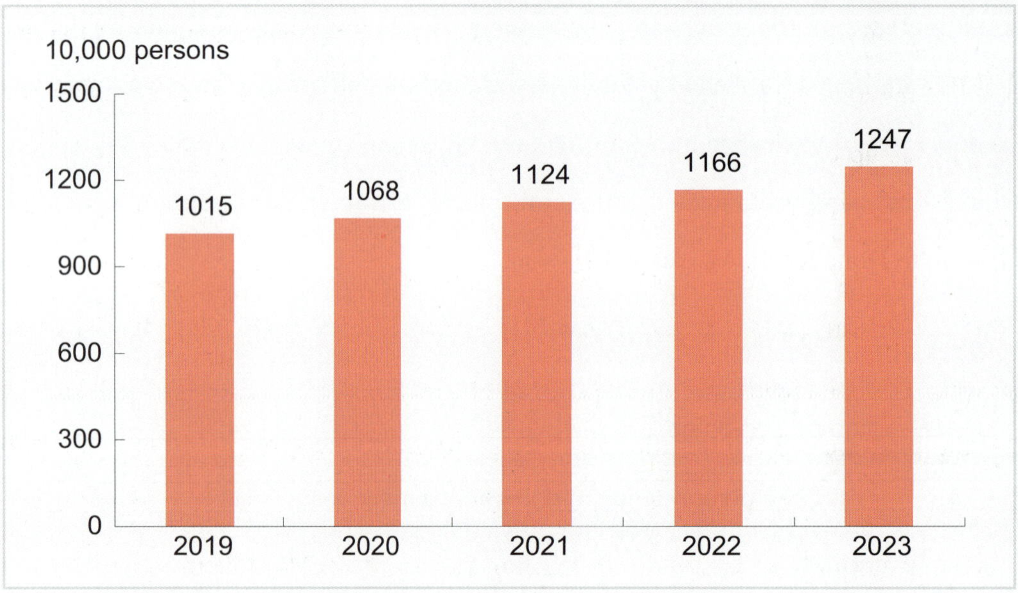

There were altogether 4.593 million sports venues[77]. The sports venue area[78] totaled 4.07 billion square meters and the per capita sports venue area was 2.89 square meters. In 2023, Chinese athletes won 165 world championships in 32 sport competitions and broke 20 world records. At the 19th Asian Games in Hangzhou, Chinese athletes won 201 gold medals and a total of 383 medals, topping the gold medal tally for 11 times in a row at the Asian Games. Chinese physically-challenged athletes won 231 world championships in 45 international sport competitions. At the 4th Asian Paralympic Games in Hangzhou, Chinese athletes won 214 gold medals and a total of 521 medals, topping the gold medal tally and overall medal count for four times in a row at the Asian Paralympic Games.

75. The total number of medical visits refers to the number of people receiving medical services, including outpatient services, emergency treatment, home visits, appointment-based diagnosis and treatment, health check-up of a specific item, and health consultation and guidance (excluding health lectures and nucleic acid tests).

76. The number of hospital discharges refers to the number of inpatients discharged from hospitals in the reporting period, including those who are discharged from hospitals or transferred to other medical institutions following doctors' advice, discharged from hospitals without doctors' permission, dead or other situations. The number of people who are recovered from family sickbeds is excluded.

77. The sports venues belonging to armed forces and railway system are excluded in the census on sports venues.

78. The sports venue area refers to area used for physical training, sports competitions and physical fitness.

XII. Resources, Environment and Emergency Management

In 2023, the total supply of state-owned land for construction use[79] was 749 thousand hectares, a decrease of 2.1 percent over that of the previous year. Of this total, the land supply for industry, mining and warehousing was 175 thousand hectares, down by 11.9 percent; that for real estate[80] was 84 thousand hectares, down by 23.3 percent; and that for infrastructure facilities was 490 thousand hectares, up by 7.2 percent.

The total stock of water resources in 2023 was 2,478.0 billion cubic meters. With a decrease of 1.5 percent over 2022, the total water consumption was 590.7 billion cubic meters, of which water consumption for domestic use was up by 0.5 percent, for industrial use up by 0.2 percent, for agricultural use down by 2.9 percent, and the artificial recharge for environmental and ecological use grew by 3.9 percent. Water consumption per 10,000 yuan of GDP[81] was 50 cubic meters, a decline of 6.4 percent. Water consumption per 10,000 yuan of industrial value added was 26 cubic meters, down by 3.9 percent. The per capita water consumption was 419 cubic meters, down by 1.4 percent.

In 2023, the total area of afforestation reached 4.00 million hectares, of which 1.33 million hectares were afforested by manpower, accounting for 33.4 percent of the total. The land area improved by grass plantation[82] was 4.38 million hectares. By the end of 2023, there were 5 national parks. A total of 63 thousand square kilometers of land have been saved from soil erosion.

Preliminary estimation indicated that the total energy consumption in 2023 amounted to 5.72 billion tons of standard coal equivalent, up by 5.7 percent over that of 2022. The consumption of coal increased by 5.6 percent; crude oil, up by 9.1 percent; natural gas, up by 7.2 percent; and electric power, up by 6.7 percent. The consumption of coal accounted for 55.3 percent of the total energy consumption, 0.7 percentage points lower than that of 2022, while clean energy consumption, such as natural gas, hydropower, nuclear power, wind power and solar power accounted for 26.4 percent, 0.4 percentage points higher. The comprehensive energy consumption per unit calcium carbide by major energy-intensive industrial enterprises went down

79. Total supply of state-owned land for construction use refers to the total amount of state-owned land for construction use with the land-use right transferred, allocated or leased to units or individuals through signed transaction contracts and allocation decisions by the municipal or county governments according to annual land supply plan and in line with relevant laws in the reporting period.

80. Land used for real estate refers to the sum of land used for commercial service and for residence.

81. The water consumption per 10,000 yuan of GDP and water consumption per 10,000 yuan of industrial value added are calculated at prices of 2020.

82. The land area improved by grass plantation refers to the area of grasslands that are ecologically restored through manual grass plantation, aerial grass seeding, the quality improvement of grasslands and fencing enclosure.

by 0.8 percent, per unit synthetic ammonia up by 0.9 percent, per ton steel up by 1.6 percent and per unit electrolytic aluminium down by 0.1 percent. The standard coal consumption per kilowatt-hour of thermal power generation decreased by 0.2 percent. Accroding to preliminary estimates, the energy consumption per 10,000 yuan worth of GDP[83] decreased by 0.5 percent over that of the previous year after deducting the consumption of raw materials and non-fossil energy. The trade volume of carbon emission quotas[84] at the China Carbon Emissions Trade Exchange reached 212 million tons with a turnover totaling 14.44 billion yuan.

Figure 24: Proportion of Clean Energy Consumption in the Total Energy Consumption 2019-2023

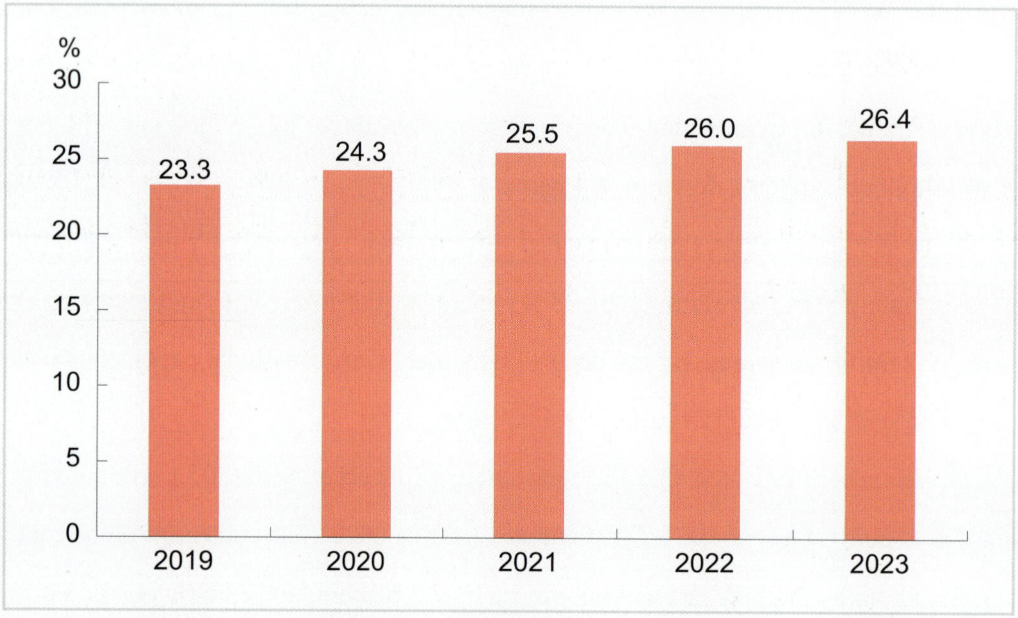

The area of offshore oceanic water[85] that met the national quality standard Grade I and II accounted for 85.0 percent; that met Grade III standard 4.5 percent; and water of Grade IV or inferior quality 10.5 percent.

Of the monitored 339 cities at prefecture level and above, the annual average concentration of particulate matter ($PM_{2.5}$) was 30 micrograms per cubic meter, up by 3.4 percent over the previous year.

Of the 326 cities subject to urban regional daytime acoustic environment monitoring, 5.8 percent enjoyed excellent environment, 69.3 percent had good environment, 23.9 percent had average environment,

83. The energy consumption per 10,000 yuan worth of GDP is calculated at prices of 2020.

84. The trade volume of carbon emission quotas at the China Carbon Emissions Trade Exchange refers to the emission quotas of greenhouse gases such as carbon dioxide allocated to major emission entities for the prescribed period at the China Carbon Emissions Trade Exchange.

85. Offshore oceanic water quality is evaluated by the area method.

0.9 percent had relatively poor environment and no city had poor environment in 2023.

The average temperature in 2023 was 10.71°C, up by 0.21°C compared with that of the previous year. Typhoons hit China 6 times in 2023.

In 2023, natural disasters hit 10.54 million hectares of crops, of which 0.98 million hectares of crops were demolished. Flood, waterlogging and geological disasters caused a direct economic loss of 245.1 billion yuan. Droughts caused a direct economic loss of 20.6 billion yuan. Disasters caused by low temperature, frost and snow made a total direct economic loss of 4.9 billion yuan. Oceanic disasters caused a direct economic loss of 2.5 billion yuan. The country recorded 11 earthquakes with magnitude 5.0 and above, causing a direct economic loss about 15.3 billion yuan. The year 2023 witnessed 328 forest fires, with 4 thousand hectares of forests damaged.

The death toll due to work accidents amounted to 21,242 people in 2023, down[86] by 4.7 percent over that of the previous year. Work accidents in industrial, mining and commercial companies caused 1.244 deaths out of every 100 thousand employees, up by 4.2 percent over that of 2022. The death toll for one million tons of coal produced in coal mines was 0.094 people, up by 23.7 percent. The road traffic death toll per 10 thousand vehicles was 1.38 people, down by 5.5 percent.

86. Data of work accidents in 2022 were verified and adjusted; and the year-on-year change for 2023 were calculated based on the adjusted data of the previous year.

Data Sources:

In this Communiqué, data of newly increased employed people in urban areas, endowment insurance, unemployment insurance, work injury insurance and skilled workers schools in secondary vocational education are from the Ministry of Human Resources and Social Security; data of foreign exchange reserves and exchange rates are from the State Administration of Foreign Exchange; data of business entities, quality inspection, the formulation and revision of national standards and qualification rate of manufactured products are from the State Administration for Market Regulation; data of environment monitoring and carbon emission trading are from the Ministry of Ecology and Environment; data of output of aquatic products, area of high-standard farmland newly developed and upgraded and area of farmland newly equipped with water-saving irrigation systems are from the Ministry of Agriculture and Rural Affairs; data of production of timber, area of afforestation, area of grass planting and improvement and national parks are from the National Forestry and Grassland Administration; data of water resources, water consumption and land newly saved from soil erosion are from the Ministry of Water Resources; data of installed power generation capacity, newly increased alternating current transformer equipment with a capacity of over 220 kilovolts and electricity consumption are from the China Electricity Council; data of volume of freight handled by ports, container shipping of ports, highway transportation, waterway transportation, new and rebuilt highways and new throughput capacity of berths for over 10,000-tonnage ships are from the Ministry of Transport; data of railway transportation, new railways put into operation, extended or new double-track railways put into operation and electrified railways put into operation are from China Railway; data of civil aviation and new civil transportation airports are from the Civil Aviation Administration of China; data of pipeline transportation are from China National Petroleum Corporation, China Petrochemical Corporation, China National Offshore Oil Corporation and China Oil & Gas Piping Network Corporation; data of motor vehicles for civilian use and traffic accidents are from the Ministry of Public Security; data of postal service are from the State Post Bureau; data of telecommunication, software revenue, and new lines of optical-fiber cables are from the Ministry of Industry and Information Technology; data of internet users and internet coverage are from the China Internet Network Information Center; data of floor space of second-hand housing online transactions, housing units rebuilt in rundown urban areas, government-subsidized rental housing and renovation of old urban residential communities are from the Ministry of Housing and Urban-Rural Development; Data of imports and exports of goods are from the General Administration of Customs;

data of imports and exports of services, foreign direct investment, outbound direct investment, overseas contracted projects and overseas labor contracts are from the Ministry of Commerce; data of finance are from the Ministry of Finance; data of newly added tax and fee cuts, deferrals and tax refunds are from the State Taxation Administration; data of monetary finance and corporate credit bonds are from the People's Bank of China; data of funds raised through domestic exchange markets are from China Securities Regulatory Commission; data of the insurance sector are from the National Financial Regulatory Administration; data of medical insurance and maternity insurance are from the National Healthcare and Security Administration; data of urban and rural minimum living allowances, relief and assistance granted to rural residents living in extreme poverty, temporary assistance and social welfare are from the Ministry of Civil Affairs; data of entitled people are from the Ministry of Veterans Affairs; data of natural science foundation projects are from the National Natural Science Foundation; data of National Fund for Technology Transfer and Commercialization, state-level technology business incubators, national mass makerspaces and technology contracts are from the Ministry of Science and Technology; data of national engineering research centers and state-level enterprises technical centers are from the National Development and Reform Commission; data of patents and trademarks are from the National Intellectual Property Administration; data of the proportion of citizens with scientific literacy are from the China Association for Science and Technology; data of satellite launches are from the State Administration of Science, Technology and Industry for National Defense; data of education are from the Ministry of Education; data of art-performing groups, public libraries, cultural centers and tourism are from the Ministry of Culture and Tourism; data of television and radio programs are from the National Radio and Television Administration; data of movies are from the China Film Administration; data of newspapers, magazines and books are from the National Press and Publication Administration; data of files are from the State Archives Administration; data of China's outbound visits are from the National Immigration Administration; data of medical care and health are from the National Health Commission; data of health supervision are from the National Disease Control and Prevention Administration; data of sports are from the General Administration of Sport; data of physically-challenged athletes are from the China Disabled Persons' Federation; data of supply of state-owned land for construction use and direct economic loss caused by oceanic disasters are from the Ministry of Natural Resources; data of average temperature and typhoons are from the China Meteorological Administration; data of areas of crops hit by natural disasters, direct economic loss caused by flood, waterlogging and geological disasters, direct economic loss caused by droughts, direct economic loss caused by low temperature, frost and snow, the number of earthquakes, direct economic loss caused by earthquakes, forest fires, areas of forests damaged and workplace accidents are from the Ministry of Emergency Management; all the other data are from the National Bureau of Statistics.

In case of any differences between English translation and the original Chinese text, the Chinese edition shall prevail.